A Pocket Guide to
BIRDS

EASTERN AND CENTRAL NORTH AMERICAN

by Allan D. Cruickshank

72 natural color photographs by Helen G. Cruickshank

78 drawings by Don Eckelberry

PUBLISHED BY POCKET BOOKS NEW YORK

To
Carl W. Buchheister and Joseph M. Cadbury

INSPIRING FRIENDS AND COLLEAGUES

A POCKET GUIDE TO BIRDS

Dodd, Mead edition published 1953

POCKET BOOK edition published May, 1954
9th printing.........................July, 1973

A Pocket Guide to Birds was previously published under the imprint
of Washington Square Press, a division of Simon & Schuster, Inc.

This POCKET BOOK edition includes every word contained
in the original, higher-priced edition. It is printed from
brand-new plates made from completely reset, clear, easy-to-
read type. POCKET BOOK editions are published by POCKET
BOOKS, a division of Simon & Schuster, Inc., 630 Fifth
Avenue, New York, N.Y. 10020. Trademarks registered
in the United States and other countries.

L

PREFACE

ONE DAY at the Audubon Camp of Maine a bird landed high in a spruce. As soon as I called it a red-breasted nuthatch several students asked, "How do you know?" Anxious to be helpful I told them the identification was extremely simple because the red-breasted is our only nuthatch with a dark line through its eye. One lady immediately said, "That is all very well, but to begin with, how do I know it is a nuthatch?"

Dr. Henry Holmes who was then dean of the Graduate School of Education at Harvard smiled and said, "Allan, remember the adage that whereas a teacher must never underestimate the intelligence of his students, he must be equally sure never to overestimate their knowledge."

Right then I realized the necessity of the most elementary approach . . . of building from the very bottom. Consequently in the last decade I have devoted as much time teaching students how to separate a nuthatch from a woodpecker and a loon from a cormorant as I have in pointing out the simplest method of separating red-breasted from white-breasted nuthatches or red-throated from common loons.

The first section of this book outlines the points I stress during every elementary field course in identification. I have limited myself to that area of the United States and southern Canada east of the Great Plains. Ornithologically speaking the hundredth meridian may be considered the dividing line between East and West. At this point many western birds become common. Anyone living in the western half of Texas, Oklahoma, Kansas, Nebraska, the Dakotas and eastern Saskatchewan should own both an eastern and western bird guide. Not all of the species occurring in the chosen area have been included. I have excluded most accidental visitors, many rarities and some species of extremely local distribution. Decisions often were influenced by my personal experiences while doing field work in every state and province covered by this book, others by the fact that I wanted an uncommon bird included to illustrate an identification technique used to separate species in some small family. I take full responsibility for the birds I have selected and those I have omitted.

For simplification I often have used phrases such as "only robin-sized auk" or "only swallow with pure white under parts." This "only" refers explicitly to birds regularly found in the area covered by this book. Likewise a term such as "breeds throughout" refers not only to the area covered by this book but also to the type of habitat which I have stated is preferred by that bird.

This book is intended primarily for beginners, non-experts and those naturalists engaged in teaching others the basic principles of bird identification. Everyone who intends to enter the graduate school of field identification should own a copy of Roger T. Peterson's **A Field Guide To The Birds.** I doubt that a field guide ever will be devised to excell it. Those wishing additional information regarding habits, nests, conservation problems or land, food and water requirements will find Richard H. Pough's **Audubon Bird Guide** and **Audubon Water Bird Guide** indispensable.

All of the families and groups of bird in this book are presented in the standard sequence now used by American ornithologists. We begin with the more primitive birds like the loons and grebes and work up to the most specialized, highly developed birds, the sparrows. Occasionally within a group, as in the owls and warblers, I have shifted species for convenient comparisons. At times I thought it expedient to head the list of birds in a unit with its most common and widely distributed representative. Moreover, wherever it would make identification easier, I have tried to separate birds into the smallest obvious field identification groups. I could see no reason to be limited by the conventional approach of presenting the crows and jays to-gether as a family when to the average person they look far more unlike than some widely separated orders such as the herons and cranes or the shearwaters and gulls. Unfortunately I found it impossible, or at least unsatisfactory, to break down some large complicated families such as the fringillidae (sparrows, etc.) into small simple clear cut groups.

Most of the common names used are those which at the time of writing are recommended by the A.O.U.'s committee on nomenclature. Wherever the name differs considerably with the one popularly used during the past decade I have included the old name in parentheses.

It is impossible to thank everyone who has contributed to this book. I would have to start with my elementary school teachers who inspired me through activities in Audubon Junior Clubs. I would have to list all of my subsequent instructors in nature study. Great tribute would have to be given to the many wonderful companions and colleagues with whom and from whom I learned the major part of my field knowledge. Many shortcuts to identification were learned from or discovered with such keen competent field companions as Robert P. Allen, John H. Baker, Carl W. Buchheister, Joseph M. Cadbury, Roland C. Clement, Howard L. Cogswell, Helen G. Cruickshank, L. Irby Davis, Ludlow Griscom, George T. Hastings, Richard A. Herbert, Joseph J. Hickey, Richard Kuerzi, C. Russell Mason, Ernst Mayr, Charles E. Mohr, Robert C. Murphy, Michael Oboiko, Roger T. Peterson, Richard H. Pough, T. S. Roberts, Walter W. Sedwitz, Alexander Sprunt, Edwin W. Teale, Charles A. Urner, William Vogt and Farida Wiley. Thanks should be given to the many thousands of students for the myriad questions which forced me to uncover or discover the simplest answers. Furthermore I must thank all of the authors and contributors to the scores of ornithological publications from which I have obtained endless information during the last thirty years. Even though I have been fortunate enough to study in the field almost all of the birds occurring annually in the United States and Canada I have drawn freely from the literature in order to present as thorough a picture as possible.

Some went far out of their way to help me with this volume. **Woman's Day** kindly permitted the use of the natural color photographs which were taken for them by my wife. I wish to thank Farida Wiley, Juliet Kellogg and Joseph Cadbury, three experienced teachers and field ornithologists, for going over the entire manuscript and offering valuable suggestions. Don Eckelberry's magnificent illustrations speak for themselves. They show the usual beauty, imagination and accuracy characteristic of all work done by this gifted artist. I am indebted to John Dearborn for permission to use his excellent diagram of the topography of a bird. Herbert Alexander, Raymond Bond, Edward H. Dodd, Jr., Ralph S. Palmer and many others were most helpful. Above all I am indebted to my wife to whom I frequently turned for advice. She acted as my secretary, checking and typing the entire manuscript and reading proof. Without her encouragement and aid this book never would have been completed,

ALLAN D. CRUICKSHANK
ROCKLEDGE, FLORIDA

Contents

HOW TO USE THIS BOOK

1. If you wish to look up a bird whose name you already know, refer to the index at the back of the book.

2. If you see a new bird closely resembling one you already know, turn to the page describing the bird you know, as species with which it could be confused usually are mentioned.

3. If you see a bird that obviously belongs to a major group or family (duck, owl, pigeon, sparrow, etc.) you already know, turn to the summary for that particular group.

4. If the bird appears entirely different from any you have seen before, look over the visual key to the major groups on pages 10-17 and undoubtedly you will be able to decide which picture most closely resembles your unknown bird. Then read the summary for that group of birds.

5. The foundation on which all bird identification rests is the ability to place a newly discovered bird in its specific family or group. This is not as difficult as it may seem at first. Almost everyone knows many major types (swans, ducks, owls, pigeons, sparrows, etc.). The beginner should read the introductory descriptions for each major group. Once one grasps this classification, the identification of most birds becomes quite simple. As in every other subject the beginning is the most difficult.

BINOCULARS

IF AT ALL possible one should buy a reliable make of binoculars, preferably a prism model with central focusing, wide field and at least six power magnification. To insure sufficient light the objectives (front lenses) should have a diameter in millimeters at least five times the power of the glass. Thus a six power binocular should read 6x30 or more. Remember a six power binocular will bring the bird six times closer and often make distinguishing field marks six times more obvious. For the serious student binoculars are indispensable.

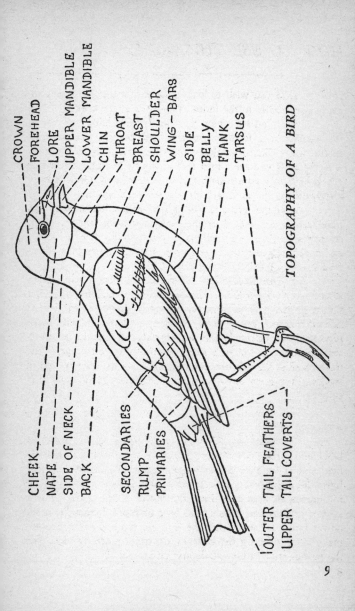

CROWN
FOREHEAD
LORE
UPPER MANDIBLE
LOWER MANDIBLE
CHIN
THROAT
BREAST
SHOULDER
WING – BARS
SIDE
BELLY
FLANK
TARSUS

CHEEK
NAPE
SIDE OF NECK
BACK
SECONDARIES
RUMP
PRIMARIES
OUTER TAIL FEATHERS
UPPER TAIL COVERTS

TOPOGRAPHY OF A BIRD

9

BIRDS USUALLY FOUND ON, OVER OR NEAR LARGE BODIES OF WATER

Most frequently they are seen in flight and appear rather gull-like. All except the gulls, terns and osprey are strictly coastal or oceanic.

Man-o'-War Bird (p. 49)

Gannet (p. 45)

Osprey (p. 79)

Gull (p. 125)

Shearwater (p. 40)

Jaeger (p. 123)

Tern (p. 129)

Petrels (p. 42)

Skimmer (p. 131)

BIRDS USUALLY FOUND ON OR NEAR WATER

Most of these have a goose-like or duck-like shape.

Loon (p. 37)

Auk (p. 133)

Goose (p. 58)

Anhinga (p. 47)

Cormorant (p. 46)

Ducks (p. 60)

Swan (p. 57)

Grebe (p. 38)

Pelican (p. 43)

BIRDS USUALLY FOUND AROUND SWAMPS, MARSHES, MUDFLATS OR SHORELINES

In flight the legs of all except the smallest birds in this group extend beyond the tip of the tail.

Heron (p. 50)

Ibis (p. 55)

Gallinule (p. 86)

Kingfisher (p. 144)

Sandpiper (p. 93)

Phalarope (p. 122)

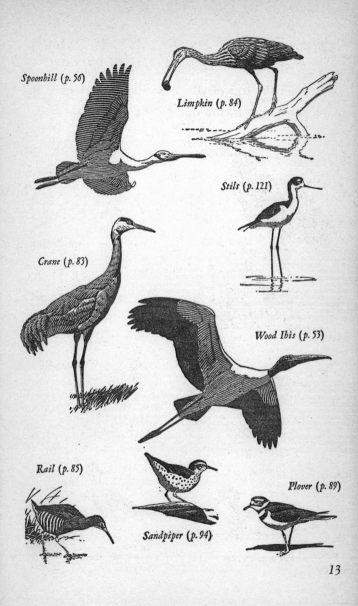

Spoonbill (p. 56)

Limpkin (p. 84)

Stilt (p. 121)

Crane (p. 83)

Wood Ibis (p. 53)

Rail (p. 85)

Sandpiper (p. 94)

Plover (p. 89)

13

HAWKS AND OWLS

Some owls have conspicuous ear-tufts, some do not; some are larger than a crow, some small as a robin.

Golden Eagle (p. 76)

Bald Eagle (p. 77)

Osprey (p. 79)

Harrier (p. 78)

Accipiter (p. 73)

Vulture (p. 70)

Buteo (p. 74)

Owl (p. 137)

Falcon (p. 79)

Owl, smallest bird on this page,

BIRDS FREQUENTLY SEEN FEEDING ON THE WING

All except the swift and some goatsuckers habitually perch in trees and bushes.

Goatsucker
(p. 140)

Swift (p. 142)

Gnatcatcher (p. 168)

Waxwing (p. 171)

Swallow
(p. 152)

Warbler (p. 186)

Flycatcher
(p. 147)

Hummingbird
(p. 143)

is approximately the size of Goatsucker above.

BIRDS FREQUENTLY SEEN ON THE GROUND

Most of these birds habitually perch in
trees and bushes.

Warbler (p. 179)

Thrush (p. 165)

Jay (p. 154)

Mockingbird (p. 162)

Sparrow (p. 197)

Blackbird (p. 191)

Pigeon (p. 134)

Starling (p. 173)

Pipit (p. 170)

Lark (p. 150)

House Sparrow (p. 190)

Chicken-like Bird (p. 81)

Crow (p. 155)

Pigeon on this page is slightly

BIRDS USUALLY SEEN IN TREES OR BUSHES

Woodpeckers, nuthatches, creepers and sometimes titmice, wrens and certain warblers habitually explore trunks, branches and dead stumps.

Kinglet (p. 168)

Oriole (p. 194)

Tanager (p. 195)

Vireo (p. 175)

Cuckoo (p. 136)

Shrike (p. 172)

Warblers
← (p. 184 & 188) →

Creeper (p. 160)

Nuthatch (p. 158)

Woodpecker (p. 145)

Wren (p. 161)
larger than Cuckoo above.

Titmouse Family (p. 157)

IDENTIFICATION

THERE IS ONLY one way to learn to identify birds in the field and that is to go out often and observe them. There are, however, ways to cut down considerably the length of time needed to recognize these lively, interesting and often elusive creatures.

Too often beginners take the difficult road to bird identification. They try to count the number of white spots on the tip of a robin's tail and the red stripes on the breast of a male yellow warbler. In other words they mistakenly believe they must memorize all the colors in great detail. If this were true, in most cases the poor beginner would have to learn the plumage of males, females, immatures and the various stages of individuals changing from summer to winter dress. Such a gigantic task would be enough to discourage almost anybody.

Fortunately most of this attention to details is unnecessary. In the identification of most birds some characteristic shape or posture, some nervous action, some simple but distinctive pattern is enough to be conclusive.

IDENTIFICATION OF DISTINCTIVE
GROUPS OR FAMILIES

ONE OF THE FIRST objectives is to learn the distinguishing characteristics of the common groups or families of birds. How does one separate a loon from a cormorant, a swallow from a swift, a woodpecker from a nuthatch, a warbler from a vireo? I prefer to use the term 'distinctive groups' rather than families, because in some cases the major field characteristics which distinguish a group of birds will be shown by all members of an order, in others by members of a family, and in still others only by those of a genus. Some groups are so unique that they cannot be confused with any other, while in some the obvious external differences are so slight that extreme caution in identification is required.

Recently I led a class of students on a field trip in a boat off the coast of Maine. A double-crested cormorant swimming to port brought forth much discussion. Some called it a loon, others insisted it was a cormorant. It is true that the light was very poor and colors did not show up clearly. It is equally true that superficially a loon and a cormorant look very much alike. But whereas the loon has a heavy, stocky neck and holds its head and thick, pointed bill virtually parallel to the surface, the cormorant has a long, snaky neck and holds its head and rather slender hooked bill tilted upward—a good separation point over a quarter of a mile away. Once these distinctions were pointed out even the beginners had no difficulty separating cormorants from loons.

Another day near New York City a group of observers discovered a bird walking up, down and around the trunk of a dead tree and periodically hacking away at it. Some immediately called the bird a woodpecker. The more experienced students said it was a nuthatch, yet when I asked someone to give one reason why the bird could not be a woodpecker, most of the students found it difficult to answer. The only necessary fact was the way the bird walked headfirst down the trunk, a feat no woodpecker could perform. In addition, a nuthatch walks easily on a trunk and never braces its tail against the tree for support while a woodpecker usually climbs jerkily and always uses its tail as a prop.

In the annotated list that follows this introduction, I have given the distinctive features of all the major groups of birds occurring in Eastern North America and I advise the beginner to learn these as quickly as possible. The ability to place a bird in its family or group is the foundation upon which all identification rests. Preceding the description of each group there is a picture of a species typical of the unit. Careful study of this illustration will go far toward acquainting the beginner with the major characteristics of that entire group of birds.

IDENTIFICATION BY SIZE

THE SIZE of a bird is an important item in identification. One usually can see whether it is very large or unusually small, but determining the size of the intermediates is often more complicated than one might imagine. Most bird books indicate the size in length, but since this measurement is taken from a dead bird resting on its back and measured from the tip of its bill to the tip of its tail it is often misleading. A species like the scissor-tailed flycatcher having a long tail is given the impressive length of 15 inches, whereas its body size is no longer than an eastern kingbird's listed as only 9 inches in length. Moreover, a heavy, round, bulky bobwhite measuring approximately the same as a slender catbird surely gives one the wrong impression.

The use of terms such as small, medium and large are all relative and often carry little significance unless compared with something else. Thus it is advisable to select a few widely known birds and use these as measuring sticks. If one says the bird is slightly larger than a common crow it means much more than if one merely states the bird is large.

Taking into consideration shape as well as length, I have attempted to compare the size of each species with one of the birds in the following list. Most of these standards are birds the reader already knows, or certainly will know within a few months of field observations. The following lengths represent average-sized birds: song sparrow 6¼ inches; robin 10 inches; domestic pigeon 13 inches; bantam hen 17 inches; common crow 18 inches; mallard 24 inches; herring gull 24 inches; Canada goose 36 inches; great blue heron 46 inches; mute swan 58 inches.

The beginner should be warned that at any distance size is often very deceptive. A ring-billed gull standing near a herring gull looks distinctly smaller, yet an immature alone on a sand bar requires extreme care for positive identification. Likewise the downy woodpecker is a pocket edition of the hairy woodpecker, but fifty feet up in a tree, the size of a single bird often is puzzling and one must rely on the quality of the note or length of the bill for identification.

IDENTIFICATION BY COLOR

ONE SHOULD not attempt to group all birds of one color together. First of all, it does little good to compare a brown bittern with a brown duck, grouse, wren, thrush or sparrow as the shapes, mannerisms and other features are so different that no one could confuse these birds with one another. Furthermore many birds possess a great variety of colors and the complications in grouping them satisfactorily are tremendous.

Some birds, however, are identified quickly by color. A black bird with showy red shoulder-patches is certainly a redwing, a bright-red bird with very black wings and tail a scarlet tanager, a yellow bird smaller than a song sparrow with black wings and tail an American goldfinch. Moreover one often can separate quickly some closely allied species by color characteristics alone. The least and semipalmated sandpipers look very much alike. One of the quickest ways to separate them is to look at the legs, yellowish in the least, black in the semipalmated. With experience one learns to look for such definite simple identification marks. All such easy clues are listed in the main text.

IDENTIFICATION BY SHAPE

As WAS pointed out in the case of the cormorant and loon, merely a silhouette impression sometimes is sufficient to separate birds in different orders. In fact, this technique is used to separate birds even within a single small group. One day as a bird flew rapidly over our boat I shouted, "Who'll name that?" One gentleman glanced up and immediately called it a barn swallow. The girl next to me was impressed by the quick identification and wanted to know how it was made.

21

Since the bird was against the sun she felt sure the observer could not have seen the dark-blue back, the salmon under parts, the white spots on the tail feathers. No indeed, yet the identification was easy because the observer had learned to recognize swallows by their size and graceful airy buoyant flight, and even in that poor light he could see the long, forked tail. Since the barn swallow is the only member of its family in the United States with a long, forked tail that was the only point necessary for identification.

There are numerous facts that a silhouette may reveal and one should train himself to notice automatically any outstanding character. What about the build, posture, legs, tail, bill, head? In many cases this will enable one to separate even two very similar birds by some slight but distinctive feature. Throughout the annotated list one will find simple clues for separating birds that beginners often confuse with one another. Here are but a few examples:

BUILD. Loons are long-bodied while grebes are short-bodied. A shrike is large-headed and heavy-set, a mockingbird slender throughout. A starling is chunky, a cowbird slim and well-proportioned.

POSTURE. The mute swan usually swims with its neck curved in a graceful S-shape whereas the whistling swan habitually holds its neck straight and stiff. A nighthawk perches lengthwise and horizontally on a limb, an owl crosswise and upright.

LEGS. The legs of a nuthatch are obvious, those of a creeper seldom visible. In flight the legs of a white pelican extend just beneath the tail, those of a wood ibis trail far behind.

TAIL. The tail of a barn swallow is deeply forked, that of a tree swallow only slightly forked, while the cliff swallow's tail is almost square. The blue jay has a long tail, the kingfisher a short one. A pheasant's tail is long and pointed, a prairie chicken's short and rounded.

BILL. The shrike with its thick slightly hooked bill need not be confused with the mockingbird whose bill is slender and pointed. The bufflehead's bill is short and thick, the hooded merganser's long, slender and saw-toothed.

HEAD. A cardinal's head is crested, a summer tanager's rounded. A horned owl's head has ear-tufts, a barred owl's is round and smooth. The canvasback's profile is long and gradually sloping, the redhead's almost round.

One just beginning bird study might consider this a great deal of information to absorb, but remember one usually begins by observing a few common birds in his immediate neighborhood. He can learn easily the means for identifying these local species. The first few are the most difficult. Each subsequent discovery becomes easier to identify . . . . and in a short time one finds himself concentrating on the simple one-point clue that separates a certain bird from all others with which it might be confused. The main thing is to realize the advantage of this system; of being able to identify a species simply by the color of the legs, the tilt of the bill or the shape of the tail! Do not let yourself be side-tracked to some haphazard system, even though at first it may seem easier. One using a typewriter for the first time might believe the one finger hunt-and-peck-method to be the simplest, but one who learns the correct touch system soon leaves the one-fingered advocate far behind.

IDENTIFICATION BY ACTIONS

Now LET us examine a case where some characteristic action or mannerism comes to one's aid. We walk down a woodland road and see a flycatcher perched on a low branch. We know it is a flycatcher not only by its upright posture but by its actions. It suddenly darts from the branch, catches an insect and returns to its favorite perch. Soon it dashes out again and catches another insect and returns. It is a typical flycatcher but what species is it? Then we note that each time the bird lands it flips its tail up and down. It must be a phoebe for that is our only flycatcher which habitually flips its tail. Similar identifying characteristics are given for other species throughout the descriptive text.

The beginner can spend less time memorizing a mass of details concerning plumage color and concentrate on learning these characteristic shapes, these tell-tale actions. Sparrows hop but pipits walk. A waterthrush teeters while an ovenbird walks daintily. An osprey plunges after fish feetfirst whereas a gannet plunges headfirst. A mallard generally feeds by tipping-up, a red-breasted merganser by diving.

The shape and mannerisms of some birds are not distinctive enough to be described readily. The points are so subtle that one has to watch the bird over and over until its diagnostic features unconsciously are memorized. I always attempt to give my students some easy means of identification, yet sometimes I am at a loss to explain how I know that a bird flying over is a given species. One example is a cedar waxwing in flight. Sometimes as I see one flying, I casually say, "There is a waxwing." Invariably someone wants to know how I knew. Even now I cannot list any easy means of identification. I could say the bird has a crest (but this is not noticeable in flight). I could say it has a yellow band on the tip of its tail (but maybe I did not see that). I might say the high, trilling lisp was what gave away the identity of the bird (but maybe I did not hear that). Yet I knew it was a waxwing! The only explanation is that after years of birding I unconsciously have memorized some delicate, indescribable but very definite shape and action of the waxwing that makes identification easy.

The following situation may help the beginner understand. Let us imagine we are sitting at the edge of a large pasture. A quarter of a mile away a girl walks across a ridge and you say: "There goes my sister." Now I turn to you and ask, "How do you know?" That sounds like an easy question, yet the chances are you are unable to give a definite answer. At that distance you cannot see the color of her eyes, the shape of her nose, the tint of her hair—yet you are sure it is your sister. Certainly you are, because since childhood you have been watching your sister, you unknowingly have memorized her particular form, some distinctive way of walking, some subtle mannerism that enables you to identify her a quarter of a mile away. So it is with many birds. To be quick and accurate at bird identification one must go out of doors often, be observant, allow the shapes, mannerisms and patterns of each species to impress themselves on his mind.

IDENTIFICATION BY PATTERN OR FIELD MARKS

IN MANY species the color arrangement is too complex to memorize, yet some simple pattern or field mark often is enough to be distinctive—so distinctive that in two very similar birds even a split-second glimpse may be enough for positive identification. As an example, a cuckoo dashes across a New York road and disappears into a thicket. All the experienced observers are sure it is a cuckoo because they already have learned to recognize the extremely long slender build of these birds. But which cuckoo is it? In that fleeting glimpse we could not see the color of the bill, nor the arrangement of spots under the tail. But the rufous flash we saw in the wing told us it was a yellow-billed cuckoo because the black-billed would be uniformly dull-brown and never would show a rufous flash in the wings.

Similarly how helpful it is to know that a scoter with a white stripe in its wing has to be a white-winged scoter, a kinglet with a ring around its eye has to be a ruby-crowned kinglet, a vulture with a white patch under each wing-tip has to be a black vulture. With experience one learns to look for these conclusive marks.

IDENTIFICATION BY FLIGHT

THE FLIGHT of many birds is distinctive. Some species are easier to identify in the air than when they are perched. The hawks offer such an example. A peregrine falcon has long, pointed wings and a steady dashing flight while the Cooper's hawk has short rounded wings and progresses by repeating a few rapid wing-beats and a sail. When starting to fly a merganser taxies along the surface seaplane fashion, but a mallard jumps straight out of the water. A crane always flies with its neck fully extended, a heron habitually folds its neck back on its shoulders. A turkey vulture glides with its wings tilted upward whereas a bald eagle glides with its wings on the horizontal.

RANGE AND SEASON OF OCCURRENCE

THE BEGINNER should become familiar not only with the normal range of a bird but also with the normal season of its occurrence. The boy I met outside of Los Angeles studying birds with the help of a field guide designed for eastern observers certainly was working under difficulties. It is a tremendous help to know that the only hummingbird one is apt to encounter over most of the eastern United States is the ruby-throated hummingbird. It is equally helpful for a New England observer to know that he should not expect to see a brown-headed nuthatch, a Bewick's wren or a Bachman's sparrow, although a straggler might occur on rare occasions. How helpful it is to know that a Franklin's gull is extremely rare along the eastern seaboard and that the laughing gull is equally rare in the interior.

Likewise a knowledge of the season in which a bird occurs is of immense importance. I recall how as a boy I spent much time following song sparrows through the thickets near our summer farm in Massachusetts hoping one would prove to be a fox sparrow. If only I had known that the fox sparrow does not breed in the eastern United States and its occurrence in summer would be accidental! How helpful it is to know that a snow bunting, tree sparrow or redpoll does not occur in the United States in summer; that a cliff swallow, scarlet tanager or wood pewee does not occur in winter. Similarly it is an advantage for a New England student to know that a brown thrush seen in winter is almost certain to be a hermit thrush, a wren in a snow-coated ravine undoubtedly a winter wren and a wintering buteo almost certainly not a broad-winged hawk! Beginners are advised to acquire the nearest local bird list for study and reference. Many states have large, handsome volumes describing the bird life within their boundaries. In addition many museums, societies and local bird clubs have excellent regional lists. Get in touch with your local Audubon Society or write to the National Audubon Society, 1130 Fifth Avenue, New York 28, New York, for advice.

HABITAT PREFERENCE

EVERY BIRD student quickly discovers the important role of food, cover and water requirements in bird study. He soon realizes that most birds are very particular as to where they will nest, and many species are just as particular as to the kind of country they will frequent even outside of the breeding season. Some species are not as discriminating as others. Moreover during migrations birds often are forced to stop off in habitats they would not ordinarily choose. But it is the normal picture that is most important. One quickly learns that it is ridiculous to look for a meadowlark in deep woods and just as foolish to look for a Swainson's (olive-backed) thrush in a wide meadow. Likewise one discovers that a seaside sparrow demands salt marshes, that a brown creeper prefers woodlands, that a bobolink wants extensive meadows. It becomes obvious then that if one wishes to see as many different species as possible he must visit as many different types of habitat as possible. As one progresses in bird study he often uses the habitat as an added clue to some identification. Thus in a marsh, a song sounding somewhat like that of a chipping sparrow but slower and more metallic surely belongs to a swamp sparrow. A bird in a northern spruce forest singing like a hooded warbler is surely a magnolia warbler. A medium-sized brownish owl flushed from the center of an extensive marsh is undoubtedly a short-eared owl. Small shorebirds alighting on the broad expanse of the ocean are probably phalaropes.

When man clears away a woodland to make a new field he

27

exchanges red-eyed vireos and ovenbirds for meadowlarks and vesper sparrows. If he fills in a marsh to make a town park, he replaces rails and marsh wrens with robins and chipping sparrows. If he neglects a meadow and allows it to become covered with bushes, he loses savannah sparrows and bobolinks but gains chestnut-sided warblers and catbirds. But one should not take this to mean that man's destruction or change of a habitat can do no harm. If a very specialized and limited type of country is destroyed, man can do much harm to the bird life of a region. Many communities have a mania for draining marshes. As these steadily disappear throughout the country the population of rails, bitterns, gallinules and ducks in some regions shrinks alarmingly low.

This habitat study is as fascinating as it is important. Many complex questions arise and any serious student will have an interesting time delving into the problems. Why should the swamp sparrow breed commonly in almost all fresh water marshes in Westchester County, New York and yet be virtually absent from most apparently similar marshes on Long Island just across the Sound? Why should the clapper rail demand salt water marshes in which to breed, while the almost identical king rail is practically as insistant on a fresh water habitat? In the annotated list I have described the habitat preferred by each species.

IDENTIFICATION BY CALLS AND SONGS

ANYONE interested in the out of doors certainly wants to learn bird calls and songs. Not only are they beautiful and add much to one's full enjoyment of hours afield, but they are of tremendous help in determining quickly which birds are present. Some people are astonished to hear that the experienced bird watcher makes a large part of his identification by ear. Hearing a bird is just as definite and reliable a means of identification as seeing it. In some cases it is even more reliable! A good example of this is in the two crows of the eastern United States. A small specimen of a common crow and a large specimen of a fish crow are virtually alike in size, build, color and actions. A sight identification would be extremely questionable. But let a common crow give one of its calls (a variety of well known caws) or the fish crow one of its calls (a hoarse cräää-cräää or a staccato că-ă) and a positive identification can be made easily by one who knows both calls well. Another example comes with three small flycatchers, the least, alder and Acadian. These three birds look so much alike that I could place an example of each on a tray and, unless they were extremely typical specimens, I could not accept unequivocally a visual identification from three feet distance, even though five of the best field ornithologists in the country were making the guess! The chances of error would be too great unless the specimens were carefully measured. If this is true of birds on a tray placed in front of five authorities, one can see that it would be just as risky in the field, although it must be admitted that locality and habitat would be of great help in a field guess. I never have accepted a sight record of any of these three flycatchers unless an experienced student heard the bird call. Then the identification becomes reliable. The least flycatcher delivers a simple, dry chebéck, the alder flycatcher says phé-beeo, the Acadian flycatcher gives a sneeze-like kazzeek!

Since songs are of such help in field work, how can one learn the voices of the various species? There is only one way and that is to go afield often, hear the songs and calls over and over again, and be serious in devising a system that will enable you to remember each. There is no substitute for field observations. When more phonographic and tape recordings are produced, repeated playing of these will be of tremendous assistance. No amount of human music, symbols or word descriptions will help a beginner to go afield and identify songs. First he must hear the song and discover the species singing it. Then, and only then, will the books on bird songs be useful in presenting him with a system for retaining the song in his mind. Naturally it will save a great deal of work and time if one can go afield with someone who knows all of the common bird songs, especially with one who can offer concrete suggestions as to how to remember them. There are three different systems which the majority of bird watchers use: music, symbols and word descriptions.

MUSIC: First is the musical approach wherein the student knows enough music to try to write each song on the musical staff. For certain simple songs this is excellent. Thus the black-capped chickadee and the white-throated sparrow might be represented in this manner:

black-capped chickadee

The bird sings one octave higher.

white-throated sparrow

The bird sings two octaves higher.

The student of music can have a great deal of fun interpreting in this way and undoubtedly can learn much about bird songs. But there are many drawbacks to this approach. First, one must have a thorough knowledge of music. Secondly, most birds do not sing according to our musical scale. They may use intervals even smaller than quarter tones in pitch, while their rhythm may be so irregular and erratic that musical measures become meaningless. Moreover screams, croaks, trills, squeaks and many other bird sounds simply cannot be written musically.

SYMBOLS: Another widely used system is the use of symbols. Dr. Aretas Saunders who is the leading authority in this field calls it musical shorthand. In this school dots, dashes and lines are arranged to approximate the length, pitch and spacing of a bird's song. Once one has had some experience in the field, this technique can be of real help in keeping records of bird songs. Thus the loud, clear call of the bobwhite may be interpreted as:

The song of the tufted titmouse may be symbolized thus:

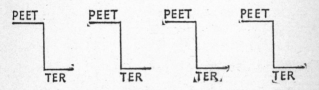

The song of the parula warbler:

FRRRRRRRRUP (*INSECT-LIKE BUZZ*)

Any student who is anxious to learn all the techniques involved is urged to study Aretas Saunder's **A Guide to Bird Songs.**

WORDS: The third and most popular system is the use of words, phrases, or descriptions which catch the spirit, rhythm and quality of a song. At first this may sound ridiculous, but after twenty years with students in the field I still believe it is the one that helps the beginner most. A new tune coming over the radio is retained more quickly if some catchy words are connected with it. Such birds as the bobwhite, killdeer, whippoor-will, phoebe and the chickadees distinctly say their names. Moreover when an eastern towhee sings, let someone tell you it says **drink your tea** and for the rest of your life each towhee

31

will say distinctly **drink your tea.** Likewise the yellowthroat asks in a lively fashion **which is it? which is it? which is it?** The ovenbird calls **teacher teacher teacher teacher teacher.** I have included many of these word suggestions in the annotated list which follows.

Naturally the birds do not say these words but since it sounds that way, the system works and that is what counts. It is true that there is much variation and that each bird has its own individual voice, but each species has a distinct quality, a characteristic rhythm, a typical song. It is not without significance that someone in New York tells you the chestnut-sided warbler says **Good-morning to dear teacher,** someone in Massachusetts claims it says **I wish to see Miss Beecher,** while a farmer in Maine is sure it sounds like **I'm very pleased to meetcha!** Notice all have caught the length and rhythm of the typical chestnut-sided warbler's song and that the conclusive identifying inflection at the end is emphasized by three very similar sounding words—teacher, Beecher, meetcha.

There is something in a bird's voice that is unmistakable even though it is indescribable. We never have any doubt as to whether our father, mother, sister or brother is speaking over the telephone. The minute the radio is turned on we recognize a familiar voice like Lowell Thomas's or Vaughn Monroe's no matter what he says or what he sings. Let someone play middle C on a flute, then on a violin and no one would have any trouble deciding which instrument was used first. Likewise with birds an indescribable but distinctive quality often aids the experienced student to separate two very similar songs.

I can not agree with those who object to the simple word system because it does not allow for all the variations in a bird's song. Too much worry about minor variations only confuses the issue. One might produce a volume full of scholarly, accurate details of variations in the songs of each species but for the inexperienced field student it would be just as useless and bewildering as a book that described a bird's color feather by feather instead of by major patterns.

Songs with clear, simple whistled notes like those of the

yellowlegs or white-throated sparrow are most accurately represented on the musical scale. Some insect-like buzzes or trills like those of the parula warbler are most accurately represented by a combination of words and symbols. Many like the killdeer, phoebe, and chestnut-sided warbler are most easily remembered by the use of human words. Others like the chipping sparrow are best described by comparison to well-known sounds.

I recommend that the student go beyond these systems, group together songs that confuse and analyze the differences. In each set of similar songs pick out the one most familiar and use it as the standard for comparison. Thus in analyzing birds with songs somewhat resembling that of a robin, a beginner might find a chart like the following extremely helpful.

ROBIN GROUP

ROBIN: A lively, cheerful, musical, whistled song usually made up of phrases with two or three notes; cheer-up cheerily cheer-up cheerily cheer-up, etc.

SCARLET TANAGER: A shorter, slower, harsher, higher-pitched song; cheer-up cheerily, cheer-up cheer-up. Notes burred, sound as though the bird were humming and whistling at the same time—a robin with a sore throat!

SUMMER TANAGER: Not as short and harsh as a scarlet tanager's, not as clear and lively as a robin's; has a wider range of pitch.

ROSE-BREASTED GROSBEAK: A sweet, bubbling, mellow, robin-like song with much swing and practically no pauses; Oh what joy. I'm bubbling o'er with bubbling joy.

RED-EYED VIREO: Two to four note, robin-like phrases delivered slowly, deliberately, incessantly. Seems to ask a question, then answer it.

SOLITARY VIREO: Sweeter, slower, higher-pitched than a red-eyed vireo's song. Notes frequently slurred together, the periodic, peculiar inflection toweeto is diagnostic.

33

YELLOW-THROATED VIREO: Slower and more buzzy than the red-eyed vireo's; see-me I am here. How are you? Harsh and slurred, sounds as though the bird were whistling and humming at the same time—a vireo with a sore throat.

YELLOW WARBLER GROUP

YELLOW-WARBLER: Sweetest and most musical of the three; Sweet sweet sweet sweeter-than-sweet.

REDSTART: Weaker, higher-pitched, more lisping; often alternates between two sets of phrases of different quality; see-see-see see sée and chewee-chewee-chewẹe.

CHESTNUT-SIDED WARBLER: Louder and clearer than the other two with a rising inflection at the end; I'm very pleased to meetcha!

CHIPPING SPARROW GROUP

CHIPPING SPARROW: A simple, unmusical trill all on one pitch. Resembles noise of a small toy sewing machine.

SLATE-COLORED JUNCO: A slower, more musical, tinkling sewing machine (in summer usually in conifer or mixed woodlands).

SWAMP SPARROW: A sweeter, stronger, slower, more metallic sewing machine sometimes delivered on two pitches simultaneously (usually in swamps).

WORM-EATING WARBLER: All on one pitch like the chipping sparrow's but faster and more buzzy (usually on wooded slopes).

PINE WARBLER: More musical sewing machine, varies more in pitch, moving a tone or two up and down (in summer, usually in pine woods).

MYRTLE WARBLER: Louder, more musical with upward or downward trend in pitch at end (summer song usually heard in northern conifer or mixed woodlands).

PHOEBE GROUP

EASTERN PHOEBE: Pheebee, voice quality, not a clear whistle.

BLACK-CAPPED CHICKADEE: Pee-bee, a clear, sweet whistle, second note a tone or two lower than the first. (Chickadee whistles it, phoebe says it).

CAROLINA CHICKADEE: Pee-bee, pee-bee (four notes rather than two as in the black-capped.

EASTERN WOOD PEWEE: Pee-wee or pee-a-wee. Plaintive, dropping in pitch, then rising part way up again.

YELLOW-BELLIED FLYCATCHER: Pĕrwee. Short, slurred upward, like abrupt wood pewee.

AMERICAN GOLDFINCH: Swee-seee. Sweet, clear, canary-like, slurred upward.

LOONS
Gaviidæ

Common Loon

THESE large, long-bodied, goose-shaped birds are essentially aquatic. They generally float low in the water, swim powerfully, slip beneath the surface with scarcely a ripple and often travel speedily underneath for long distances at a time. On the water they most closely resemble cormorants but have shorter, stouter necks and carry their long, sharply-pointed bills almost parallel to the surface. It is conceivable beginners might confuse loons with grebes, geese and large ducks. Our eastern grebes are decidedly smaller, shorter-bodied and carry their relatively longer, slimmer necks much more erect. Compared with geese, loons float lower in the water, have long sharply pointed bills instead of short blunt ones, are shorter-necked, and regularly dive. The only ducks with which loons could be confused are silhouetted mergansers, but all of these except the male common are crested. He is smaller and has a slim, slightly-hooked bill instead of a heavy sharply-pointed one. Since loons are practically helpless on land they seldom are seen on the ground far from the water's edge. Like most diving birds they generally have to run along the surface before flying. In the air they look hunch-backed, hold their necks

37

fully extended and slightly drooping, and carry their large feet protruding beyond an absurdly short tail. They appear to droop at both ends! This flight is comparable only to that of the grebes, but grebes are distinctly smaller, most have white patches on the wings, and travel with an even more obvious droop to the neck. Somewhat similarly shaped birds like the cormorants, geese and mergansers have noticeable tails and hold their necks straight out or tilted slightly upward.

COMMON LOON. Our most widely distributed loon; only species normally seen on most inland waters. Size of small Canada goose. Summer adults: head and most of neck glossy black, back checkered black and white, under parts white, bill black. Winter and immature: dark-gray above, white beneath, gray bill. Voice: loud mournful yodeled hoo-loooooo and wavering maniacal ha-ha-ha unmistakable. Breeds from Arctic south to northern border of U.S. Migrates throughout; winters chiefly along coast.

RED-THROATED LOON. Red-throated birds infrequently seen in U.S. Others similar to winter common loons but decidedly smaller, paler, profile snakier, back speckled with white, upward slant of lower mandible giving much thinner bill uptilted appearance. Breeds mostly in Arctic; winters chiefly on U.S. tidal waters south to c. Florida.

GREBES
Colymbidæ

GREBES are nearly tail-less, duck-like birds with long, slender necks and pointed bills. They are smaller than loons, look shorter-bodied and carry their relatively longer, slimmer necks more erect. If the neck and body of a loon outline two sides of a rectangle those of a grebe more closely suggest a square. The slender, erect necks of our large grebes in conjunction with their long, thin, sharply-pointed bills quickly separate them from cormorants, geese and ducks.

Horned Grebe (Winter)

Grebes are popularly known as hell-divers. They spend most of their life in the water, ordinarily diving to escape rather than flying. As danger approaches they sink progressively lower, as it nears they slide quickly under the surface or abruptly vanish as though jerked from beneath. Like loons they are practically helpless on land, and must run along the surface of the water before flying. Their flight is somewhat labored, and the extended neck droops, giving the appearance of a bird ready to collapse. The only other birds of similar shape that droop their necks are the loons, but loons are bigger and unlike the large grebes do not have extensive white patches in the wings.

RED-NECKED GREBE (HOLBOELL'S). Largest eastern grebe, slightly smaller than mallard. In any plumage only dark-necked grebe with yellow bill. In flight two white patches on wing obvious. Summer adults with red neck, white cheeks and throat, black crown and back of neck, rarely seen in East. Winter and immature: mostly grayish; dark crown, white crescent on side of face. Breeds south to Minnesota, s. Ontario; winters chiefly along coast, uncommonly south of North Carolina.

HORNED GREBE. Half mallard size, slender bill. Summer adults with gray back, rusty neck and sides, buffy ear-tufts and black head, uncommon over most of East. Winter and immature: black of crown, back of neck, and back contrasts sharply with pure white cheeks, neck and under parts. Voice: rippling trill. Breeds south to Nebraska, Wisconsin, s. Ontario; migrates throughout; winters chiefly on Great Lakes and along coast.

PIED-BILLED GREBE. Only grebe with thick bill. Half mallard size. Mostly brown; often floats with rear end high revealing white under tail-coverts. Summer adults have black throat, black ring around bill. Voice: loud, resonant cow cow cow cow-cow-cow cow-uh cow-uh cow-uh. Generally confined to fresh or brakish water. Breeds locally throughout; winters chiefly south of New Jersey, Indiana.

SHEARWATERS
Procellariidæ

ALTHOUGH shearwaters are common summer visitors to our off shore water they are so partial to pelagic haunts that they are seen only infrequently from the land. They all have a characteristic tube on the nose but it is seldom noticeable on the wide expanse of the ocean. These gull-like birds hold their long, narrow wings so rigidly that they look like miniature gliders. Periodically they give several rapid flaps, but mostly glide, bank and skim with great speed in the troughs or just above the waves, often traveling for hundreds of yards without a single flap. In some areas black skimmers are referred to as shearwaters, but the long blade-like bill of the skimmer dispels any question of relationship. Despite widespread belief to the contrary jaegers with their angled wings and dashing hawk-like flight bear little resemblance to the stiff-winged gliding shearwaters.

SOOTY SHEARWATER. Only shearwater with dark under parts; bird appears all black at a distance. Smaller than a herring gull (size of laughing gull). Dark sooty-brown except for whitish wing-linings. Breeds in southern part of Southern Hemisphere.

Greater Shearwater

GREATER SHEARWATER. Slightly larger; upper parts brownish-black, under parts white; **sharply defined dark cap contrasts with white throat, neck and lower face; white patch at base of tail; thin black bill.** Breeds on islands of Tristan da Cunha in South Atlantic.

CINEREOUS SHEARWATER (CORY'S). Largest shearwater, only one with yellow bill. Some almost herring gull size. Grayish-brown above, white beneath; gray of head merges into white throat. Paler and less contrasty than greater shearwater, bill much thicker. Most of our visitors breed on islands off Portugal and n.w. Africa.

STORM PETRELS *Hydrobatidæ*

Wilson's Petrel

STORM PETRELS, called Carey-chickens by American fishermen, are small, swallow-like seabirds almost the size of a robin. Our species are dark with conspicuous white rumps. The tube on the nose seldom is visible on the ocean. Petrels expertly skim and flutter just above the waves, so close their webbed feet frequently touch the water. They rarely come near enough to the shore to be seen from land. Occasionally swallows are seen flying over the ocean, but none of our species has a white rump, and all except the purple martin are decidedly smaller. Dark plumaged black terns could cause only momentary confusion for they are larger with sharply pointed bills, dark rumps and much silver-gray in the wings.

LEACH'S PETREL. Mostly dark-sooty; brownish band across wing, tail deeply forked, black feet seldom visible. Flight distinctive; erratic bounds and long glides with frequent shifts in direction. Breeds south to islands off New England coast, flying around nesting grounds only under cover of darkness, where it sings a soft, purring, rhythmic Pleased-to-meet-cha. How-do-you-do?

WILSON'S PETREL. Slightly smaller, blacker; yellow feet project beyond short, unforked tail. Wings shorter; flight not so bounding; bird flutters and glides, often pattering feet on surface as though walking on the water. Regularly follows ships. Summer visitor from Southern Hemisphere.

PELICANS
Pelecanidæ

ALMOST everyone recognizes pelicans. They are very large, ponderous water birds with huge, flat bills, enormous throat-pouches, and comical, unforgettable faces. On the water they float high and swim about with grace and speed. In flight as well as at rest the head usually is drawn back on the shoulders, the bill often resting on the breast. Their wings are long, broad and rounded, their tails short but wide. These grotesque, almost voiceless birds frequently travel in long lines and V's slowly flapping and sailing in leisurely rhythm, often skimming just a foot above the water. They soar with grace, the white pelicans sometimes circling in compact flocks at tremendous heights.

WHITE PELICAN. One of our largest American birds, size of mute swan. Weight often 15 lbs., wing-spread 8½ ft. Mostly snowy white; throat-pouch yellow, primaries and

White Pelican

half of secondaries black. Scoops up fish while swimming instead of plunging. Accidental over most of East; some breed on Texas coast; some winter along Gulf of Mexico and in Florida.

BROWN PELICAN. Slightly smaller; weight often 8 lbs., wing-spread 6½ ft. Adult: body mostly dark-brown, wings and back silvery, much of head and sides of neck yellowish-white. In winter head and neck white. **Immature; chiefly brown above**, white beneath. Plunges headlong into water after fish. Habitually perches on posts and boats in southern harbors. Confined almost exclusively to coast from North Carolina to Texas.

GANNETS
Sulidæ

Gannet

THESE BIRDS look like large, powerful gulls but have longer, thicker necks, longer, heavier bills, and longer, pointed tails. At all times they appear to taper at both ends. In flight the bill usually is tilted downward. They are master gliders, giving a few rather rapid wing-beats between each sail. When fishing they plunge from a height (sometimes 100 feet up) headfirst into the water, the resulting splash often visible over a half mile away. In winter off southern coasts one might confuse them with diving brown pelicans, but pelicans are much more ponderous and have broad, rounded wings instead of long, slender, pointed ones.

GANNET. Only species normally seen in U.S. Twice bulk of herring gull, wing-spread 6 ft. Adult: snowy-white, much black on wing-tips, yellow wash on head. Immatures: vary

45

from uniform brown to splotched black and white. Breeds on Canadian islands; common transient along coast; winters off shore, chiefly south of Delaware.

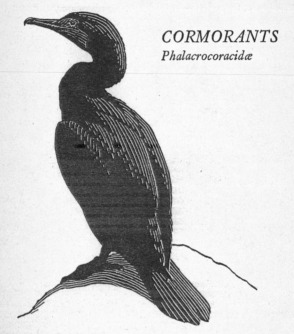

CORMORANTS
Phalacrocoracidæ

Double-crested Cormorant

BECAUSE of their shape and habit of flying in long lines and V's, cormorants in the air often are mistaken for geese. Their black coloration, quicker wing-beat and silence proclaim them cormorants. To beginners, individuals in flight might resemble loons, but since their entire body tilts upward and the tail is prominent they are easily distinguished from the virtually tail-less loons which appear to droop at both ends. At a distance when the larger cormorant size is not obvious, its slower wing-beat and lack of silvery wing-linings will separate it from a black duck. Cormorants perch upright with their necks usually in an S-shaped position, often with wings widely outstretched. They are experts in the water, diving from the surface with ease and traveling long distances beneath in pursuit of fish. On the water they most closely resemble loons, but their necks are snakier, their bills hooked at the tip, their heads tilted distinctly upward. Geese float higher and have short, blunt bills instead of long, slender ones. All ducks except the male common (American) merganser are either too small, broad-billed or crested for comparison. The male common merganser is mostly white; in silhouette it is obviously smaller, slimmer, shorter-necked, and does not tilt its head up cormorant style. Even our largest grebes are smaller, shorter bodied and hold their much more slender sharply pointed bills horizontally.

DOUBLE-CRESTED CORMORANT. Smaller than Canada goose. Adult: black with yellow-orange pouch. Immature: browner, whitish under parts but dusky belly. Only common, widely distributed cormorant in East. Breeds very locally from Canada to Gulf of Mexico; winters chiefly along coast, few north of Virginia.

COMMON CORMORANT (EUROPEAN). Larger, heavier, thicker-necked. Adult: white throat-patch behind yellow chin-pouch; in spring white patch on flanks. Immature: under parts often white all the way to tail. Breeds south to Nova Scotia; winters along coast, rarely south of New York.

ANHINGAS
Anhingidæ

THERE ARE four species of anhingas in the world, only one occurring in this country. They resemble cormorants but are much slimmer and have longer tails, snakier necks, smaller heads and thinner, sharply pointed bills. Like cormorants they perch upright often with wings spread wide. They

Anhinga

are experts in the water, diving from the surface with scarcely a ripple and often traveling underneath for long distances at a time. When alarmed they float low, frequently with only neck and head above the water. They often soar. In flight the long tail usually is fanned, the slender neck fully extended, the long glides periodically interrupted by several rapid flaps.

ANHINGA (SNAKE-BIRD, WATER-TURKEY). Smaller than Canada Goose, decidedly slimmer. Male: glossy black; conspicuous white patches, streaks and spots on fore part of wing. Female and immature: mostly black; head, neck and breast tawny. Prefers fresh water swamps and marshes. Breeds north to Missouri, North Carolina; winters chiefly in southernmost states.

MAN-O'WAR-BIRDS *Fregatidæ*

Magnificent Frigate-Bird

THESE spectacular, gregarious birds probably have a greater expanse of wing (7½ ft.) in proportion to their body weight (3½ lb.) than any other bird in the world. Their long, narrow, angular, pointed wings, long, deeply-forked tail, long, hooked bill and expertness at soaring and gliding make identification easy. In flight the tail frequently is folded and appears extremely long, slender and sharply-pointed. Man-o'war-birds roam tropical seas ordinarily staying within easy reach of land. They snatch fish from the surface with amazing agility and regularly rob gulls, terns and other water birds of their catch.

MAGNIFICENT FRIGATE-BIRD. Male: black with orange-red throat-pouch. Female: black with white breast. Immature: black above; entire head and under parts white. Rare in East away from coastal waters of Florida and Louisiana. Swallow-tailed kite is smaller, has white instead of black wing-linings, a very short bill instead of a very long one.

HERONS
Ardeidæ

Great Blue Heron

These long-legged, long-necked waders ordinarily are seen in shallow water, at the water's edge, or in marshes patiently searching for fish, frogs and other aquatic animals. In some areas, however, the larger species often frequent pastures and meadows to feed on insects and mice. They have long, narrow, feathered heads, long, straight, sharply-pointed bills, and long, slender toes. Most of them are extremely slim and graceful, many carry showy plumes on the head, breast and over the lower back (especially at breeding time). The thick, broad-based bill of the wood ibis and the sharply-decurved cylindrical bills of the true ibises quickly differentiate them from herons. If in flight for any distance, herons fold their necks back on their shoulders and trail their long legs horizontally behind. Their wing-beats are slow, measured and deep. Although the larger species superficially resemble the stockier, blunter-billed cranes and are often erroneously called so, they are not even closely related to that family. In flight cranes and ibises fly with their necks fully outstretched instead of retracted. Most herons are gregarious, the largest roosts and breeding colonies often containing thousands of birds. After the breeding season many wander northward, some of the southern egrets often straggling as far north as Canada.

GREAT BLUE HERON. Our only large blue-gray heron (excluding rare Florida Wurdemann's). Common and widely distributed; erroneously called crane by many. 4 ft. tall, 6 ft. wing-spread, brown wash on neck. Adult: whitish head; long, dark ear-tufts; plumes on breast and back. Voice: deep, hoarse walk; throaty croaks and squawks. Breeds locally throughout; winters chiefly in southern states, few north to Massachusetts, Great Lakes.

COMMON EGRET (AMERICAN). Only large, yellow-billed white heron with black legs and feet. Slightly smaller than great blue. Breeding birds have long, delicate plumes draped over lower back. Voice: hoarse croaks. Breeds in southern states, locally north to New Jersey, s. Wisconsin; winters chiefly south of Cape Hatteras.

SNOWY EGRET. Only white heron with black legs plus golden slippers. Half size of preceding with slender black bill, recurved plumes. Feeds actively, shuffling feet to stir up food, even running after small fish. Immature: yellowish wash on back of legs. Voice: bubbling wă-lă-lă-lă; hoarse croaks.

51

Breeds in South, some north to Long Island, Missouri; winters chiefly along coast south of Cape Hatteras.

TRICOLORED HERON (LOUISIANA). Only dark, gray-blue heron with contrasting white belly. Half size of great blue; very slender even for a heron, delicate gray-brown plumes draped over back. Immature: browner, especially on neck. Voice: wild croaks. Breeds in coastal areas from s. New Jersey to Texas; rarely wanders north of New Jersey; winters chiefly south of Cape Hatteras.

LITTLE BLUE HERON. Only dark, slate-blue, slim heron (often looks black). Half size of great blue; slender head and neck. Dark, two-toned bill; dark legs; maroon head and neck. Immature: white; black-tipped, bluish bill; **gray-green legs and feet.** (Snowy egret has black legs, yellow feet, thinner black bill; shuffles feet while feeding.) Changing birds: blotched slate-blue and white. Voice: hoarse croaks. Breeds in southern states, some north to New Jersey, rarely farther; summer wanderings sometimes north to Canada (usually white birds in July, August); winters chiefly south of Cape Hatteras.

GREEN HERON. Only dark, stocky, crow-sized heron (often appears black). Legs rather short for a heron. Actions deliberate. Stretches neck, raises crest and flicks tail when alarmed. Adult: dark, blue-green; neck chestnut, legs yellow or orange. Immature: browner, more streaked. Voice: loud, hollow keou; sharp kuk-kuk-kuk. Breeds almost throughout; winters chiefly along coast, most south of Georgia.

BLACK-CROWNED NIGHT HERON. Night herons are most active from dusk to dawn. They are stockier, shorter-legged, thicker-necked, more deliberate than most herons. They are half the size of a great blue. In flight the black-crown looks very broad-winged, feet barely project beyond tail. It is our only whitish heron with contrasting black back. Wings gray, back and crown black, thick bill black, legs and feet yellow or salmon. Immature: gray-brown, spotted and streaked with

52

white; dusky-yellow legs. (Bittern richer yellow-brown; in flight shows conspicuous black wing-tips.) Voice: hollow wŏk and qua. Breeds throughout; winters locally north to Ohio, Massachusetts.

YELLOW-CROWNED NIGHT HERON. Only medium-sized, blue-gray heron with black and white head. Yellow wash on crown seldom obvious. More slender, longer-legged, shorter-billed than black-crown. Immature: darker than black-crown, back more finely speckled, bill shorter and thicker, legs longer (in flight projecting well beyond tail). Voice: hollow wăk. Breeds chiefly in South, some north to Massachusetts, Missouri; winters north to Florida.

AMERICAN BITTERN. Only medium-sized buffy heron. Essentially a terrestrial marsh dweller; secretive, freezes with bill pointing up. Stocky, short-legged. Streaks on breast, black stripe on neck, black wing-tips. (Young night herons grayer, lack black wing-tips.) Spring song: hollow, liquid, oft-repeated, pumping **gump-a-gook** or **plum puddin'**; alarm; hoarse gŏk-gŏk-gŏk. Breeds throughout; winters chiefly in southern states; rarely north of Delaware, s. Ohio valley.

LEAST BITTERN. Smallest heron, average length 1 ft. When alarmed points bill up. Confined chiefly to dense swamp vegetation; difficult to see, difficult to flush. Mostly yellow-brown; black on crown, back and wing-tips. Voice: harsh kĕk kĕk kĕk; soft wă wă wă. Breeds north to s. Quebec, Great Lakes, Minnesota; winters north to Georgia.

WOOD IBIS
Ciconiidæ

In SPITE of its name this bird is not an ibis but is a unique stork in a sub-family of its own. It is a long-necked, long-legged, white bird about the size of a great blue heron. Unlike herons it has a dark-gray, naked head, and a long, dark, thick-based, slightly decurved bill. The tail, wing-tips and rear half of the wings are black. It feeds in shallow water, walking se-

Wood Ibis

dately, often shuffling its feet to stir up food. In flight the long neck always is carried fully extended, the long legs trailing behind the short, square tail. The bird appears to droop at both ends. There is little resemblance to the much smaller true ibises with their long slender distinctly decurved bills. The somewhat similarly shaped cranes are longer-necked, more slender-billed; they have a more sedate upright posture, fly with a diagnositc rapid upstroke to the wings, and never perch in trees.

Being gregarious wood ibises often travel in large flocks, alternately flapping and sailing in unison. Sometimes they sail majestically at great altitudes on motionless wings; occasionally they twist, turn and volplane in spectacular plunges to the earth. They occur chiefly in lowland swamps from South Carolina to Texas.

IBISES
Threskiornithinæ

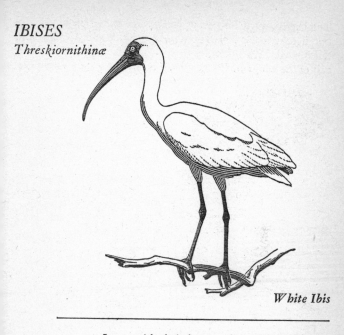

White Ibis

IBISES with their long necks and long legs superficially resemble medium-sized herons. Unlike herons they have long, conspicuously decurved, rather cylindrical bills and in flight always carry their necks fully outstretched. They have much more rapid wing-beats than herons and usually travel by alternating a few quick flaps with a sail. The V-shaped flocks, long lines and bunched formations are breath-taking as the birds rush, bank and wheel at a surprising speed on their broad rounded wings. They feed chiefly in shallow water or moist places, and usually nest in flooded woodlands or on small isolated islands. They are gregarious, some breeding colonies and roosts often numbering many thousands of birds. In some areas natives call them curlews, but curlews have shorter necks, shorter legs, more slender bills and a more uniform warmer brown plumage than any young ibis.

GLOSSY IBIS. Black-looking ibis; at close range mostly glossy-chestnut. Voice: gutteral gä-gä-gä-gä. Resident on peninsula Florida; stragglers wander north, rarely above Mason and Dixon line.

WHITE-FACED IBIS. Almost identical, but white on face all around base of bill. During the breeding season when the lores (skin between bill and eyes) of the glossy ibis turn whitish, one must be very careful with identification. Resident in coastal Texas and Louisiana.

WHITE IBIS. Only snow-white ibis. Bright-red face, bill and legs; black wing-tips. Immature: brown back and wings, white belly and rump, dusky head and neck, dull-red bill and legs. Voice: deep ŭnk-ŭnk. Breeds in low country from South Carolina to Texas; few winter north of Florida and Louisiana.

SPOONBILLS
Plataleinæ

Roseate Spoonbill

THERE are six species in this unique sub-family, only one occurring in the Western Hemisphere. Their amazing, flat, spoon-shaped bills quickly separate them from all other birds. They are almost half the size of a great blue heron; in shape, size, actions and habits most closely resembling the ibises to which they are closely related. Like ibises they have long necks and long legs; they fly with their necks fully outstretched, have much more rapid wing-beats than herons and ordinarily travel by alternating a few quick flaps with a sail. They feed in the shallows, swinging their bills back and forth in the water as they walk. They are gregarious, usually nesting on isolated islands, often in colonies of herons and ibises.

ROSEATE SPOONBILL. Spoon-shaped bill and pink plumage identifies it. Average length 32 inches. Wings, belly, legs and tail mostly pink, the latter with orange caste. Shoulders and tuft in center of breast usually blood-red. Neck, back and upper breast chiefly pinkish white; naked head greenish-gray with dark ear-patches and red eyes. Immature: white; some with obvious pink wash on wings. Voice: taciturn; low grunts. Breeds locally on Texas coast, few in s. Florida; casual visitor north to South Carolina.

SWANS
Cygninæ

Whistling Swan

SINCE childhood almost everyone in this country has seen pictures of swans in books and live specimens on park ponds. They look like over-sized geese with graceful necks, as long as or longer than the entire body. They are powerful swimmers easily outdistancing the strongest oarsman. Swans are essentially aquatic, feeding mostly in shallow water by tipping-up or merely immersing their long necks and heads and feeding from the bottom. On land they look ungainly, walking with a slow awkward gait. In flight they often travel in lines and V-formations, moving fast with slow, powerful wing-beats and with extremely long necks fully outstretched. Our species are snowy-white with wings that stretch 7 feet from tip to tip. At a distance a white pelican could be confused with a swan but the short neck and huge bill of the pelican quickly distinguish it. In flight the pelican has much black on the wings and holds its short neck drawn back rather than fully extended.

MUTE SWAN. Introduced from Europe to our park ponds and private estates. Escapees now live in wild state around New York City region. Length often 5 ft., weight sometimes 25 lbs. Snowy-white; **black knob on orange bill.** Immature: brown wash; **dusky bill** without knob. More graceful on water than whistler, neck usually curved, wings often arched over back. Voice: whining **whee-you;** loud hiss; in flight surprisingly loud musical **here here here** of wings quite different from soft swish of other swans.

WHISTLING SWAN. Slightly smaller. Snowy-white; **black bill without knob,** yellow spot between eye and bill. Immature: brown wash; **dull flesh-colored bill.** Vociferous; loud, musical **woo-hoo woo** audible a mile away. Breeds in Arctic; migrates in definite flyways; winters chiefly on coastal bays from Maryland to North Carolina.

GEESE
Anserinæ

Our wild geese are similar enough to the geese found in farmyards and on park ponds to be recognized immediately as members of the same sub-family. Most are larger and heavier than ducks with longer necks and shorter, stouter bills. Unlike most ducks, both sexes look alike. Furthermore the majority are much more terrestrial, regularly walking around graz-

Canada Goose

ing like cattle, even in dry fields far from water. Although most geese are less aquatic than ducks, they swim buoyantly and fast. They habitually feed from the bottom of shallow water by tipping-up or simply immersing their necks and heads. In the air steady powerful wing-beats make them move much faster than it appears. They fly with their necks fully extended, often traveling in spectacular V-formations, normally honking as they go. At all times, even in silhouette, their short, blunt bills prevent any confusion with the long-billed loons and cormorants.

CANADA GOOSE. Most common, widely distributed goose in East. Our birds usually 35-43 inches in length, 7-14 lbs. in weight. Black head and neck with conspicuous white chinstrap from ear to ear conclusive. Brown above, brownish-gray below; light chest, white all around base of dark tail. Very noisy: loud, resonant ää-ronk ää-ronk audible half mile away. Most birds breeding in U.S. east of the Mississippi probably only semi-wild. Common transient almost throughout; locally common winter resident.

AMERICAN BRANT. Looks like mallard-sized Canada goose, but black breast, small white spot on neck instead of chin-strap, whiter under parts, quicker wing-beats. Very noisy; gutteral **gr-r-r-r-onk.** Breeds in Arctic; migrates to Atlantic coast; winters chiefly on tidal bays from Long Island to North Carolina. Rare in U.S. away from tidal waters.

SNOW GOOSE. Our only snow-white goose. Smaller than Canada goose; black wing-tips, pink bill. Rusty stains often present on face. Immature: dusky wash to plumage. Taciturn; nasal honking **wonk.** Breeds in Arctic; migrates in narrow flight lanes; winters chiefly along Gulf from Louisiana to Texas and on Atlantic bays from Delaware to North Carolina.

BLUE GOOSE. Only white-headed dark goose in East. Slightly larger than mallard. Mostly blue-gray; with white head, neck and tail-end. Head often stained with rusty. Immature: brownish-gray with white tail-end, **dark bill and feet.** Voice: honking **wonk.** Breeds in Arctic; migrates through Mississippi Valley; winters chiefly on coastal Louisiana and Texas.

DUCKS

Our wild ducks are much more slender and graceful than the barnyard varieties. Most people have seen enough of them either in the wild or on park ponds to know what they look like. They are smaller than geese with flatter bodies, shorter necks, shorter legs and generally longer, broader bills. Unlike geese the males of most species are much more

Black Duck

brightly colored than the females. In most the drakes desert the females during the summer and molt into a temporary drab, female-like eclipse plumage. In flight their necks are fully extended and their quick, steady wing-beats carry them at a great speed. Their spectacular angles, lines, skeins and bunches flying over are among the most thrilling sights in nature. At a distance in silhouette some species resemble either loons, grebes, cormorants, coots or gallinules but even a quick study of the family descriptions will enable an observer to see the differences. Since most people know the mallard I have used it as the standard for size comparison, taking into consideration shape and weight as well as length.

It is a great aid in identification to divide our ducks into the three following sub-families: surface-feeding ducks, diving ducks, mergansers.

Pintail

ALTHOUGH not confined to weedy shores, small ponds, streams and marshes they normally prefer to be in such habitat. They frequently feed on land, walking about with a slight waddle. More often they feed in shallow water by dabbling, or tipping-up and gathering food from the bottom. Although they can dive they seldom do so. When rising from the water or land they spring directly into the air without any preliminary run. Many of them have an attractive rectangular patch called a speculum on the rear edge of the wing.

MALLARD. Average length 2 ft., weight 2½ lbs. Most abundant duck in world, common on many park ponds. **Male: only broad-billed duck with conspicuous white neck-ring separating bright-green head and neck from rusty breast.** Mostly gray; bill yellow, tail-end black and white. Female mottled brown; **whitish tail, orange and black bill,** speculum (wing-patch) blue bordered in front and back with white. Vociferous: throaty **quack** or **quack-wack-wack-wack.** Breeds chiefly from Great Lakes westward (semi-wild birds locally common in northeast; winters mostly south of Massachusetts, Iowa.

BLACK DUCK. Mallard size. Sexes alike; dusky-brown (often looks black); gray-brown head, straw bill, violet speculum, brown or red legs and feet. In flight white wing-linings distinctive. Vociferous: throaty quack or quack-wack-wack-wack. Breeds south to North Carolina, Ohio, west to Minnesota; winters almost throughout (uncommon in West).

GADWALL. Slightly smaller, slimmer than mallard. Male: smooth, dusky-gray; black around base of tail, silvery wing-coverts, gray-brown head, white speculum (sometimes hidden). Female: mottled brown; straw-colored bill and feet. white speculum. In flight both sexes show white belly, white square on rear edge of wing. Voice: high quack; deep wok-wŏk. Breeds chiefly in West, south to Kansas, east to Wisconsin, some to North Carolina, Delaware Bay and Long Island; winters chiefly in southern states.

PINTAIL. Mallard size. Alert, graceful, slender with long, thin neck. Male: only surface-feeding duck with long, pointed tail. Mostly pale gray; head brown; breast, fore neck and stripe extending into head white; black under tail-end. Female: pale mottled brown; slightly pointed tail, gray bill, white border to rear of brown speculum. Voice: hoarse quack; mellow whistle. Breeds southeast to Iowa, rarely farther; winters chiefly near coast, few north of Long Island, Louisiana.

GREEN-WINGED TEAL. Half mallard size; rapid, erratic flight, small bill. Only native teal with no conspicuous light patch on wing. Male: brownish-gray; green patch on side of chestnut head, white crescent on side of breast, green speculum. Female: gray-brown; green speculum. (Female blue-wing has large, conspicuous, light wing-patch, heavier bill.) Voice: high quack; trilled peep-peep. Breeds southeast to Iowa; winters chiefly in South, few north of Long Island, Arkansas.

BLUE-WINGED TEAL. Slightly larger than green-wing, quickly separated from it by large, pale-blue (often looks white) patch on front of wing. Male: mostly brown; white crescent on face, black and white around tail-end. Female: brown (size, light wing-patch distinctive). Voice: soft quack; rapid peep. Breeds south to New Jersey, Ohio, Kansas; winters north to South Carolina, Louisiana.

AMERICAN WIDGEON (BALDPATE). Smaller than mallard. **Male: only surface-feeding duck with white crown.** Mostly pinkish-brown; large white patch on fore part of wing, green patch on side of gray head, black and white around pointed tail. Female: rich-brown; gray head and neck, **large white patch on fore part of wing.** Voice: alarmed qua-ack; mellow whistled whee-whee whu. Breeds east to Minnesota, Nebraska, rarely farther; winters chiefly in southern states, seldom north of Long Island, Louisiana.

SHOVELER. Decidedly smaller than mallard. **Only duck with long, broad, spoon-shaped bill.** Male: breast and back mostly white, **sides and belly rich chestnut,** head green, large pale-blue patch (often looks white) on fore part of wing. Female: mottled brown; large pale-blue patch on fore part of wing **(larger size and huge bill separate it from blue-winged teal).** Taciturn; weak quack; throaty cook-cook-cook. Breeds southeast to Iowa, Wisconsin, locally to Delaware; winters chiefly near coast, rarely north of Long Island, Louisiana.

WOOD DUCK. Decidedly smaller than mallard; **head crested, bill short.** Male: **our most versi-colored, iridescent duck;** mostly chestnut on breast and neck, white on chin and throat, green and purple on head, pale-buff on sides, bronzy-blue and green on back, numerous white stripes. **Female: crested; mostly bronzy-brown; white around eye.** In flight both sexes hold their heads high and show long, square, dark tail, dark back and chest, white belly, thin white edge on back of dark wing. Voice: plaintive hoo-eek; shrill crek-crek. Prefers flooded woodlands, habitually perching in trees. Breeds locally throughout; winters chiefly in deep south, rarely north of Virginia, Arkansas.

Canvasback

THESE are the ducks most frequently seen in great rafts on large bodies of water. Some occur in narrow streams or in marsh pools but even these species seldom walk far from the water's edge. Their feet are so far back that they stand more erect than, and do not walk as well as, their surface-feeding relatives. Instead of tipping-up they expertly dive, often going down great distances in pursuit of fish, or for marine animals and plants on the bottom. When taking off they must run over the surface of the water to work up enough speed for flight.

REDHEAD. Slightly smaller than mallard. **Male: our only diving duck with high-domed red head.** Mostly gray; black chest, dark tail-end, dark tip to bluish bill. Female: mostly brown; **high, rounded head, light area around base of bill.** In flight both sexes show **broad, gray wing-stripe.** Breeds

65

chiefly northwest of Iowa; winters very locally, mainly along coast from New York to Texas.

RING-NECKED DUCK. Decidedly smaller than mallard. **Male: black back plus chalky-white crescent separating black chest from gray sides conclusive.** Black head high-domed (almost crested) glossed purple; two white bands across bill; dark-red neck-ring seldom visible. Female: dark-brown, darkest on high crown and back; pale near base of bill, **white ring around eye and front of bill.** In flight both sexes show **broad, gray wing-stripe.** Breeds chiefly in central Canada southeast to Wisconsin; locally to Maine, New Brunswick; winters mostly in southern states, rarely north of Massachusetts, Tennessee.

CANVASBACK. Size of mallard. **Male: only red-headed duck with long, flat, gradually sloping profile,** (female mergansers have crested rusty heads; male redhead high, abrupt forehead). Mostly white; dark-red head and neck, long, broad-based, black bill; black chest and tail-end. Female: **same characteristic profile;** mostly gray; red wash to head and neck; dusky chest and tail-end. Breeds southeast to Minnesota, Nebraska; winters chiefly along coast from New York to Mexico.

SCAUP DUCK (BLUE-BILL). Smaller than mallard. **Male: appears white with black head, neck, chest and tail;** when closer one notices green or purple gloss on head, fine gray markings on body, blue bill. Female: mostly brown; **broad white band on face around base of bill.** In flight both sexes show **broad, white stripe down rear edge of wing.** Beginners should not try to separate lesser and greater scaup as it is extremely difficult and often impossible even for experienced observers. Breeds chiefly from Arctic to Nebraska; winters mostly on Great Lakes and tidal bays south to Florida.

COMMON GOLDENEYE (AMERICAN). Frequently called whistler because wing-action often produces loud, musical whistle. Slightly smaller than mallard; short neck; large, high-domed triangular head. Male: mostly white with dark back and tail; dark glossy green head; large round white spot between eye and bill. Female: mostly gray; brown head, white collar and belly. In flight both sexes look short-necked, large-headed; show large white squares on wings. Breeds south to n.e. Maine, New York, Minnesota; winters chiefly in northern states, very few to Florida.

BUFFLEHEAD. Very small, half mallard size. Plump, short-billed, large-headed. Male: only duck with large white patch extending over top of round head from cheek to cheek. Mostly white with dark back; black portion of head glossed with green and purple. Female: dusky-brown; light breast; white spot on cheek of large, round, dark head. In flight both sexes look small, stocky, short-necked, large-headed; have rapid wing-beats; male shows much white on wings and back; female large white squares on back of wings. Breeds chiefly in w. Canada; winters mostly from Massachusetts, Illinois south to n. Florida.

OLDSQUAW. Decidedly smaller than mallard. Male: only diving duck with long pointed tail. Striking brown and white pattern, short bill. Female: dark-brown above, white below; head white with black patches; no streaming tail. Both sexes have fast, erratic flight, deep wing-beats; appear black and white with uniformly dark, pointed wings. They show much more white in winter. Vociferous: loud, nasal, baying howdoodle-do. Breeds in Arctic; winters chiefly on Great Lakes and tidal waters north of Cape Hatteras.

COMMON EIDER (AMERICAN). Large, chunky, thick-necked oceanic duck with long sloping profile. Size of mallard but much heavier. Male: our only duck with completely white back above black belly. Breast, fore part of wings and most of head white; crown black. Female: long sloping profile; rich-brown plumage heavily barred. Immature male: dusky-brown with white collar (white back, head and breast appearing with subsequent molts. Intermediates pied brown and white). This species has distinctive flight: usually low over water, head slightly drooping, bird often periodically gliding. Breeds along coast south to Maine; winters south to Massachusetts, few to Long Island.

WHITE-WINGED SCOTER. Scoters are medium-sized, stocky, short-necked, blackish ducks with characteristic rounded profiles. Very gregarious, known to us chiefly as winter visitors on tidal waters. White-winged **our largest scoter, only one with white wing-patch.** Mallard size. Male: black with orange bill, white crescent below eye, black knob above nostrils. Female: dusky-brown; two light areas on side of head. Breeds chiefly in Canada; winter visitor to Great Lakes, mostly to tidal waters north of Charleston.

SURF SCOTER. Slightly smaller than mallard. **Male: only scoter with large white patch on back of head,** thus skunk-head. Mostly black; often second white patch on forehead; conspicuous orange, yellow and white bill, large and swollen at base. Female: dusky-brown; light belly, **two white spots on side of head, large wide-based bill.** Breeds chiefly in northern Canada; winters mostly just off shore or on large coastal bays south to Georgia, few to Florida.

BLACK SCOTER (AMERICAN). Slightly smaller than mallard. Male: black; **bright-yellow knob between dark bill and forehead.** Female: dusky-brown; **whitish cheek** and belly (other female scoters have two white patches on each side of face). Breeds in Arctic; winters chiefly along coast, most north of Georgia.

RUDDY DUCK. In different sub-family from rest of diving ducks; our only duck that can not walk. Much smaller than mallard, dumpy, dark. Rapid bumble-bee flight. **Male: habitually cocks large tail upright;** mostly ruddy with black cap, white cheeks; long, wide, blue bill. (Winter: grayer, bill dull.) Female: brownish-gray; dark cap, light cheeks. Courting male utters explosive **chuck-chuck-chuck** (usually with head pumping). Breeds chiefly west of Minnesota; winters mostly on fresh water near coast south of New England.

MERGANSERS
Merginæ

Common Merganser

MERGANSERS or sheldrakes are diving ducks with slender, saw-toothed bills adapted for grasping slippery fish. They are long-bodied, the larger species almost loon-like in silhouette. Like other diving ducks they seldom walk far from the water's edge and must patter along the surface before flying. In flight they assume a characteristic taut shape, perfectly horizontal, as though stretched on a stiff, inflexible rod. Their wing-beats are astonishingly shallow and rapid, their flight swift and direct.

HOODED MERGANSER. Smaller than mallard. **Male:** only merganser with large black and white fan-shaped crest (habitually spread to expose large white triangle). Back mostly black, sides rusty; breast, belly, wing-patch white; neck, front

69

of face and crown black. Female: mostly dusky-brown; **rusty wash on dark crest,** white breast and belly; white patch on back of wing. Breeds chiefly in southern Canada, northernmost U.S.; winters locally on fresh water, most near coast.

COMMON MERGANSER (AMERICAN). Mallard size. Male: **only merganser without noticeable crest.** Mostly white with dark back, dark-green head, bright-red bill and feet, large white patch on back half of wing. Female: mostly gray with rusty crested head; **clean white throat, neck, breast** and under parts; white square on rear of wing; reddish bill and feet. Breeds south to northern rim of U.S.; winters mostly on fresh water, chiefly in northern states.

RED-BREASTED MERGANSER. Mallard size. Male: **only merganser with rusty breast, only one with conspicuously crested dark-green head.** Upper parts mostly black and white, under parts whitish; white collar, red bill and feet, large white square on back half of wing. Female: mostly gray above, whitish below; **cinnamon-brown of crest and head gradually blending into pale-gray of throat, neck, breast.** Breeds south to northern rim of U.S.; winters almost throughout (coastal states: red-breast usually on salt water, common usually on fresh).

VULTURES
Cathartidæ

Our vultures are dark, almost eagle-sized birds with small, naked, warty heads and long, thick, hooked bills. Their legs and feet though strong do not have the long, sharp claws of the closely related hawks and eagles. They are essentially carrion eaters, quickly congregating around any dead animal. Away from their nesting sites they are often gregarious. Although they look clumsy and hunch-backed when perched,

70

once in the air they are master gliders, sailing and soaring expertly, the turkey vulture with unsurpassed grace. They habitually perch on posts and dead trees, sometimes with their wings widely outstretched. Many people erroneously call them buzzards.

Turkey Vulture

TURKEY VULTURE. Our largest vulture. Length 2½ ft., wing-spread 6 ft. **Only vulture with long, slim tail.** Blackbrown; astonishingly small head, red in adults, black in immatures. **Glides with uptilted wings, tipping from side to side;** occasional flaps slow and measured. Silvery cast down rear under surface of wings. Breeds north to w. Connecticut, Minnesota; winters north to New Jersey, Ohio Valley.

BLACK VULTURE. Length 2 ft., wing-spread almost 5 ft. Blacker, stockier, shorter-tailed, broader-winged than preceding; heavier head dark even in adults. **Wings darker, white area on under surface near each wing-tip. Soars less expertly, holding wings almost horizontal,** usually interrupting each short sail with several **very rapid flaps.** Resident north to Maryland, s. Ohio, Missouri.

Bald Eagle

EVERYONE knows what hawks and eagles look like. Even though one has not observed them in the field or zoological parks, he certainly has seen them in books and paintings or on stamps and coins. They all have curved, sharply-pointed, hooked bills and powerful feet with sharp claws, this latter characteristic shared only with owls. Our American species range in size from the nine-inch sparrow hawk to the forty-inch golden eagle which has wings that sometimes spread more than seven feet from tip to tip. Singularly many species are much easier to identify in flight than they are when perched.

Some immatures are extremely difficulty to separate and must be identified with great caution. Gulls which often soar in wide circles high in the sky might be mistaken for hawks. The long, slender, pointed wings of gulls however, are unlike the broad, rounded jagged-tipped wings of most hawks. Peregrine falcons with their pointed wings have longer, slimmer tails than gulls and usually interrupt any brief soaring with periods of rapid, dashing flight.

Extensive scientific studies indicate that most of these birds are extremely useful. They are part of the natural check and balance in nature and everyone should help to eliminate the old-fashioned prejudice against them.

Field students must learn the major characteristics of the following sub-families: (although eagles and buteos belong in the same sub-family I consider them distinctive enough to present separately).

ACCIPITERS
Accipitrinæ

Cooper's Hawk

THESE slim, stream-lined hawks have short, rounded wings, long tails and small heads. Flight is normally fast, three or four rapid wing-beats preceding each long sail. They generally keep in the concealing cover of woods and thickets, dashing out to catch prey by surprise.

SHARP-SHINNED HAWK. Size of domestic pigeon. Average length 1 ft. End of tail square, sometimes notched. Adult: back blue-gray; under parts white, heavily barred with rusty. Immature: brown above, heavily streaked with brown beneath. Voice: excited kĕk-kĕk-kĕk-kĕk. Resident almost throughout; uncommon in winter in northern states and Canada.

COOPER'S HAWK. Large edition of preceding. Average length 1 1/3 ft. End of tail rounded; wing-beats slower. Since large (female) sharp-shins may be as large as small (male) Cooper's, separation often is difficult, sometimes impossible. The tail difference is obvious only when tail is folded. Voice: excited kăk-kăk-kăk-kăk. Resident almost throughout; uncommon in winter in northern states and Canada.

GOSHAWK. Largest accipiter, larger than crow. Some females nearly twice bulk of male Cooper's. Average length almost 2 ft. Adult: only accipiter with finely-barred pale-gray under parts. Gray upper parts, dark cap, white stripe over eye, dark patch back of eye. Immature: mostly brown above, heavily streaked with brown beneath. Small specimens often inseparable from large immature Cooper's; some show a more distinct eye-stripe, some are much larger. Voice: deep kŭk-kŭk-kŭk-kŭk; harsh hi-ya. Breeds south to n. New England, n. Michigan, few in mountains to Maryland; winters south to Virginia, Oklahoma.

BUTEOS
Buteoninæ (in part)

THESE large, bulky, heavy-set hawks have broad wings and wide, rounded tails, the latter normally spread fan-like while soaring. They frequently are seen high in the sky sailing in wide circles. During the breeding season the red-tail prefers dry woods, the red-shoulder moist woods, the broad-winged wooded hills.

74

RED-TAILED HAWK. Larger than crow, often 2 ft. long. **Adult: only buteo with red upper tail-surface.** Mostly dark-brown above, white below; brown streaks on sides and across upper belly. Immature: similar but tail brown above, lightly, narrowly banded with black. Voice: sputtering **keeaaarrr.** Resident throughout; rare in northernmost U.S. and Canada in winter.

Red-tailed Hawk

RED-SHOULDERED HAWK. Slightly smaller, slimmer, longer-tailed than preceding. **In flight translucent-looking light patches at base of primaries.** Adult: mostly gray and brown above; white, heavily barred with rusty below; rusty shoulders; **narrow white stripes across both sides of dark tail.** Immature: brown above, heavily streaked with brown underneath, tail less distinctly banded. Voice: wild, complaining, almost whistled **key-year.** Resident west to Great Plains; rare in winter in northernmost states.

BROAD-WINGED HAWK. Smaller than crow, some males slightly over 1 ft. long. **Adult: only buteo with equally broad black and white bands alternating across tail.** Mostly dark-brown above, heavily barred with rusty-red below. Immature: like immature red-shoulder, but smaller, more compact, only to be identified by experienced observers. Voice: high-pitched creaking **ps-eeeeee.** Breeds south to c. Texas, Florida; winters chiefly in tropics, rarely north of Florida.

ROUGH-LEGGED HAWK. Our only buteo that habitually hovers on rapidly beating wings. Larger than crow, sometimes 2 ft. long. Upper parts mostly brown; head and neck whitish, heavily streaked with dusky; breast and legs buffy; **belly black; tail white with broad dark terminal band.** In flight from below the black belly, wrist-patches and terminal tail-band are prominent. A dark phase is mostly black, in flight shows white under tail and flight feathers. Voice: loud squealing **hurry-up.** Prefers open grassy country. Breeds chiefly in Arctic; winters south to North Carolina, n. Louisiana.

EAGLES
Buteoninæ (in part)

THESE majestic hawks are quite similar in shape to buteos but they are much larger and stockier with longer wings and heavier bills. They habitually soar buteo-style. At other times their flight is direct and fast, their wing-beats deliberate and powerful.

GOLDEN EAGLE. Very large: weight often 12 lbs., wing-spread sometimes over 7 ft. **Adult: mostly blackish; white at base of tail;** golden wash on head not always noticeable. Immature: mostly blackish but **conspicuous white areas at base of primaries; dark terminal band on white tail.** (Immature bald eagle usually shows white in wing-linings, not black; might have white in tail, but never has sharply defined terminal band). Voice: harsh **keea.** Very rare east of Rockies, occurring chiefly in wildest mountain areas.

Golden Eagle

BALD EAGLE. National emblem. Approximately same size as golden eagle but wings and tail narrower, head and bill heavier. **Adult: only eagle with snow-white head and tail.** Mostly blackish-brown; very large yellow bill. Immature: mostly blackish-brown, whitish wing-linings (often white patches elsewhere). Voice: deep **kak-kak-kak;** squealing **pleek-kleek-kik-kik.** Resident locally throughout; in many areas known only as rare visitor.

HARRIERS
Circinæ

THESE marsh dwellers have long, slim bodies, small heads, long, round-tipped wings, long, square-tipped tails. They habitually fly and float just a few feet about the vegetation, their long graceful glides periodically punctuated by a few leisurely wing-beats. They usually glide with wings raised above the horizontal, tilting from side to side, periodically hovering as they hunt.

Marsh Hawk

MARSH HAWK. Larger than crow. **Conspicuous white rump in any plumage.** Adult male: upper parts pale-gray, under parts mostly white, extreme wing-tips black. Female and immature: upper parts brown, under parts streaked brown. Voice: harsh kă-kă-kă-kă; nasal whistled pe-ter pe-ter. Breeds locally throughout; winters chiefly in southern states, few north to Massachusetts, Great Lakes.

OSPREY
Pandionidæ

THIS large hawk normally is associated with water. Its wings are long, narrow and distinctly angled. It habitually hovers above the water on rapidly beating wings and dramatically plunges feet first after fish.

Osprey

OSPREY (FISH HAWK). Much larger than crow, size of herring gull. Often 2 ft. long with 6 ft. wing-spread. Dark-brown above, white below; head white with black patch across eye; black patch under wrist-joint. Voice: clear, staccato, whistled you you you; throaty guk-guk-guk; squealing, complaining shriek shriek shriek! Breeds locally throughout; winters north to Gulf States.

FALCONS
Falconinæ

THESE beautifully proportioned, streamlined hawks have large heads, long pointed wings and long tails. In

79

most species their flight is direct and dashing, their wing-beats rapid and powerful. In the breeding season the peregrine falcon prefers cliffs, the pigeon hawk conifer woods, the sparrow hawk open country with a scattering of trees.

Peregrine Falcon

PEREGRINE FALCON (DUCK HAWK). Crow size. Adult: dark slate-blue above; whitish throat and neck; dark cap and mustache; barred breast and belly. Immature; brown above, streaked below, dark mustache. Voice: harsh **kak-kak-kak-kak**; wailing **keeya**. Breeds from Arctic south to mountains of Georgia, sparsely to Louisiana; few remain in northernmost states in winter.

PIGEON HAWK. Pigeon size. Darker, more compact, shorter-tailed than sparrow hawk; flight more dashing. Male: dark blue-gray above; buffy-gray, heavily streaked below; **equally broad, alternating white and dark bands on tail.** Female and immature: dusky-brown above, heavily streaked below, white stripes across tail. Voice: harsh screaming **quick-ĭk-ĭk-ĭk.** Breeds south to northernmost U.S.; rarely winters north of Gulf States.

SPARROW HAWK. Slightly shorter than preceding, yet only half its weight. **Only small hawk with red tail or red back.** Flight normally leisurely; **habitually hovers on rapidly beating wings** with tail fanned as it scans ground below, flicks tail vigorously on alighting. Male: rufous back; black-tipped, rufous tail; gray-blue wings; spotted, buffy breast; red, blue and black hood above white throat and lower face. Female: rusty above, streaked below, rufous tail barred and tipped with black, paler hood than male. Voice: rapid **killy-killy-killy.** Resident throughout; most leave northernmost states in winter.

CHICKEN-LIKE BIRDS
Phasianoidæ

Ruffed Grouse

THESE are the wild cousins of our barnyard fowl and usually will be recognized as such. Some are as small as a robin, others as large as a turkey, but they are all plump with thick chicken-like bills, legs and feet. Although some of them spend much time in trees they are essentially terrestrial. Their strong legs and feet make it easy for them to scratch for food and enable them to run with surprising speed. Although most prefer to run and hide in order to escape, their flight is strong and direct, their relatively short, rounded wings usually making a startling whirr as the bird flushes.

RUFFED GROUSE. Size of bantam hen. Red-brown or gray-brown; **dark ruffs around neck; wide fan-shaped tail with broad black and white terminal bands.** Drums a hollow, thumping bup bup bup bup up-up-up-up-rrrrr. Prefers brushy woodlands. Resident from James Bay south to Pennsylvania, Wisconsin (locally to Ohio and Missouri), in mountains to Georgia.

PRAIRIE CHICKEN. Size of bantam hen. Mostly brown, **heavily barred; short round dark tail.** In spring male gives mournful, hollow moo-loo-moo. Prefers brushy prairies. Resident from s. Manitoba south to Arkansas, locally east to Michigan, also Texas and s.w. Louisiana.

BOBWHITE. Often referred to as quail. Small as robin, chubby, almost round, mostly brown. **Male: throat and stripe over eye white.** Whistles quoi-lee; clear Bob-white or poor Bob-white. Prefers brushy farmlands. Resident north to New England, s. Ontario, Minnesota.

RING-NECKED PHEASANT. Size of large hen but **long, pointed tail.** Male: often 3 ft. long; mostly brown, rusty and gold; **usually conspicuous white ring around neck.** Female: mottled brown; shorter tail. Voice: short, crowed cook-cook followed by drumming of wings; when flushed squawky honking like old-fashioned auto horn. Prefers brush country. Resident where introduced, chiefly from Maine, s. Ontario, s. Saskatchewan south to Maryland, Kentucky, Oklahoma.

TURKEY. Almost identical to barnyard turkey. Wild birds are slimmer and have chestnut tips to tail feathers instead of white. Voice: throaty gobble-obble-obble-obble; plaintive keow keow keow. Prefers brushy woodlands. Breeds north to Pennsylvania, s. Missouri.

CRANES
Gruidæ

Sandhill Crane

THESE large, long-legged, long-necked birds superficially resemble herons but they are decidedly stockier, have thicker, less pointed bills and their lengthened inner wing-quills curve down in a conspicuous tuft over the tips of their wings and tail. In adults the top of the head to below the eyes is covered with a dull-red, almost featherless skin. Unlike herons they fly with their necks fully extended. Their flight is distinctive; each slow downward beat of the wings is followed by a surprisingly rapid upstroke. They are terrestrial, preferring wide

83

open savannas or prairie marshes and never perch in trees. The great strides of their long legs carry them sedately yet rapidly across the ground. The wood ibis, another long-legged, long-necked bird has a shorter neck, a much longer, heavier, thick-based bill and habitually perches in trees.

SANDHILL CRANE. Only crane one can expect to see east of the Mississippi. Large as great blue heron. **Adult: uniformly gray except for red skin on head.** Immature: browner; head fully feathered. Often gather in great flocks. Voice: loud, resonant, trumpeting **k-r-r-oo k-r-r-oo** audible mile away. Prefers prairies. Unknown in most eastern states. Breeds southeast to Michigan (some in Florida and Georgia); winters in Florida and along Gulf Coast.

LIMPKIN
Aramidæ

Limpkin

There is only one limpkin. It is in a separate family of its own. It is in the same super-family with cranes and exhibits the typical crane flight wherein the neck is fully extended and each slow downward beat of the wings is followed

84

by a surprisingly rapid upstroke. The limpkin however, more closely resembles an ibis-sized (roughly crow-sized) rail and like rails prefers to skulk in marsh vegetation or feed in shallow water close to protective cover. Unlike rails it habitually perches in bushes and trees and often nests there. It has long legs, a long, thick, slightly decurved bill, a short square tail and its dark-brown plumage is speckled with white especially on the neck, breast and shoulders. The limpkin is loquacious. Wherever it occurs one is sure to hear both day and night the loud penetrating incessant wailing **krra-ow** and **krrreee-you**. In the United States this interesting bird is confined to Florida and southern Georgia.

RAILS
Rallinæ

Virginia Rail

THE popular name of marsh hen is descriptive since these chicken-like birds spend most of their time skulking in dense tangles of marsh vegetation. Their short-tailed bodies are compressed laterally enabling them to slip between closely bunched reeds. Their large, strong legs and long, slender toes carry them with great speed across the marsh. Occasionally one may be seen walking on an open mud flat, or at times swimming with head bobbing emphatically as it hurries across some small pool. They are very difficult to flush, preferring to sneak away and hide. Their flight is weak and labored as on short, rounded wings they flutter for a short distance, their feet

85

dangling just above the vegetation. Most of the time they are mere voices in the marsh yet one can readily identify them by their distinctive calls. Coots and gallinules are more aquatic and duck-like, frequently swimming on expanses of open water. The unique brightly colored forehead shields of the gallinules and the wide-based white bill of the coot set them apart.

VIRGINIA RAIL. Only rail as small as a robin having long slender bill. Mostly red-brown; gray cheeks, black and white bars on belly. Juvenile: blackish. Voice: staccato, metallic kíd-ick kíd-ick; rapidly descending yăk-yăk-yăk-yăk-yăk. Breeds south to North Carolina, Missouri; winters chiefly in South.

KING RAIL. Bantam hen-sized edition of preceding but no gray on cheeks. Voice: hollow grunting umph umph umph-umph-umph-umph on one pitch. Virtually confined to fresh water. Breeds north to Massachusetts, Minnesota; winters chiefly in South.

CLAPPER RAIL. Almost identical to king rail but grayer. Voice: harsh chattering cha-cha-cha-cha. Confined to salt marshes. Breeds north to Connecticut; most winter south of New Jersey.

SORA. Only common rail with short, thick, yellow bill. Robin size, plump. Adult: mostly dark-brown above, gray below; black face and throat. Immature: buffy, no black on face or throat. Voice: plaintive, clear ker-weeee (spring), abrupt keek; long, rapid series of rolling notes descending scale (whinny). Prefers fresh water marshes. Breeds south to Maryland, Missouri; winters chiefly south of North Carolina.

GALLINULES AND COOTS
Gallinulinæ and *Fulicinæ*

BECAUSE these rail-like birds are not as secretive as their close relatives and spend much time swimming

on the open water they are often mistaken for ducks. Unlike ducks they have thick, chicken-like bills, large forehead shields, and smaller heads which they habitually pump back and forth. They are active and lively, frequently flirting their tails, often

Common Gallinule

tipping-up on the water or diving for food. Although they prefer extensive marshlands they frequently come to land where they walk and run with the ease of a chicken. When alarmed they run quickly for cover or skitter and patter along the surface into the protection of dense marsh vegetation. They are extremely noisy, their loud cackles and grunts usually announcing their presence. Rails are less aquatic seldom swimming more than a short distance. No rail has the bright forehead shield of a gallinule or the broad-based white bill of a coot.

PURPLE GALLINULE. Only gallinule with bright-yellow legs or blue forehead shield. Half mallard size. Strikingly colored: head, neck and under parts mostly purple; back olive-green; wings blue, tinged with green; bill red and yellow; undertail area solid white. Unlike common gallinule **frequently climbs about bushes.** Voice: hen-like cackles and squawks. Breeds north to South Carolina, Tennessee; winters north to s. Florida, s. Texas.

COMMON GALLINULE (FLORIDA). The gallinule seen over most of eastern U.S. Differs from preceding in being mostly brown and sooty; having red forehead shield, white streaks on flanks, dull-greenish legs, dark patch extending up into white undertail area. Voice: complaining **cak-cak-cak-cak**, numerous chicken-like grunts and squawks. Breeds north to Vermont, s. Ontario, Minnesota; winters chiefly in southern states.

AMERICAN COOT. Stockier than gallinule with heavier head, more gregarious; ventures farther from protective vegetation. Mostly sooty-black; **white bill**, white patch under tail; tremendous lobed toes. In flight white border on rear edge of wing. Voice: loud, plaintive **kurruk kurruk**; numerous clucks and grunts. Breeds locally south to New Jersey, Arkansas (few to Florida); winters chiefly in South.

SHOREBIRDS

Spotted Sandpiper

THIS is a large, varied group, but anyone who knows a single sandpiper or plover automatically will associate and compare most allied forms with the species he already knows. Most shorebirds are waders with rounded or slightly flattened bodies, short tails, long pointed wings and long, slender legs. Practically all can walk and run speedily, their leg motion often astonishingly fast. Many are expert swimmers. The great majority prefer moist, open country stippled with pools of water. They habitually stand on one leg with the other tucked out of sight. Sometimes they even hop along on one foot which accounts for frequent reports of one-legged birds seen along the beach.

Shorebirds, at least outside the breeding season, are very gregarious, some migrating flocks consisting of thousands of birds. Some are among our most rapid fliers. They usually travel with necks fully extended, legs held horizontally behind, the larger species often in impressive lines and V-formations. Their wheeling flocks never fail to arouse admiration as they bank and twist or rise and fall with astonishing precision and co-ordination.

Beginners will find it very helpful to learn the characteristics of the following four distinct families: plovers, sandpipers, stilts and phalaropes.

PLOVER FAMILY
Charadriidæ

Killdeer

PLOVERS are plump shorebirds with large, rounded heads, short, thick necks, short, pigeon-like bills and large eyes. They are thrush-like in actions, running with head low, then snapping to attention with upright, military posture; head high, chest out, wings smartly at sides.

89

PIPING PLOVER. Only whitish plover with either black ring around neck, black-tipped yellow bill or yellow legs and feet. Smaller than robin; black patch above forehead; in flight white wing-stripe. Fall and immature: bill black (separated from snowy by yellow legs, grayer back, lack of dark ear-patch). Voice: low, plaintive, melodious, whistled peep peep-lo. Prefers sandy beaches. Breeds from North Carolina to Massachusetts, very locally to Gulf of St. Lawrence (also very locally inland); winters along coast from South Carolina to Texas.

SNOWY PLOVER. Smaller, whiter-backed than preceding with dark legs, thin dark bill, black ear-patch, only short black neck-stripe. (Piping plover always has yellow legs, grayer back, lacks dark ear-patch.) Voice: musical whistled ă-wee-ă. Prefers sandy beaches. Resident along Gulf from Florida to Texas.

RINGED PLOVER (SEMIPALMATED). Brown-backed edition of piping plover; brown cap extending over cheeks. (Killdeer much larger, has additional breast band). Voice: sweet cheer-ee. Prefers mudflats. Breeds in Canada; migrates throughout (abundantly on coast); winters along coast chiefly south of North Carolina.

THICK-BILLED PLOVER (WILSON'S). Another ring-necked plover, slightly larger than preceding; longer, thicker, black bill; paler brown upper parts, dull, flesh-colored legs. (Immature ringed plover with dark bill identified by tiny bill, yellow legs.) Voice: sharp whistled wheat. Prefers sandy beaches. Breeds along coast from Texas to Virginia, sparsely farther north; winters from Florida to Texas.

KILLDEER. Most widely known shorebird in U.S. Equally pleased with plowed fields, pastures, pond edges, mudflats, park lawns or baseball fields. Size of robin; brown above, white below, two breast-bands; long tail; rump and upper tail coverts orange-red; conspicuous white wing stripe. Vociferous; noisy kill-deer kill-deer; plaintive, rising dee-ee. Breeds locally throughout; winters chiefly south of Connecticut, Iowa.

BLACK-BELLIED PLOVER. Only pale-backed plover with black throat, breast, upper belly. Larger than robin; barred white tail. In flight white wing-stripe, black axillars (under armpit). Fall and immature: mostly pale-gray; black axillars or white tail conclusive. (Rare golden plover though quite similar at all seasons always has dark tail, pale axillars, golden-brown back, no wing-stripe.) Voice: plaintive, mellow, whistled plee-o-ee or plee-oo. Prefers open, moist ground. Breeds mostly in Arctic; migrates throughout, chiefly along coast; winters along coast, most south of Virginia.

RUDDY TURNSTONE. Robin size. Robust as plover but thinner-billed, shorter-legged. Adults spectacular: ruddy back, white head and under parts, complex black pattern across breast and up to face, orange-red legs and feet. In flight striking ruddy, black and white pattern conclusive. Fall and immature: browner (especially on head) but characteristic pattern evident. Voice: musical, chuckling chuckle-chuck. Prefers moist rocky, pebbly or sandy areas. Breeds in Arctic; migrates throughout, chiefly along coast; winters along coast, most south of Virginia.

SANDPIPER FAMILY
Scolopacidæ

UNLIKE plovers most of the sandpiper family have long, slender bills, frequently several times longer than the head. These bills may be straight as in dowitchers, up-curved as in godwits or decurved as in curlews. Most members of this family are slender with smaller heads and eyes than plovers.

AMERICAN WOODCOCK. Unique, no other shorebird so round and chunky, or with such large eyes placed high on head. Larger than robin; long, needle-like bill. Virtually shapeless, neckless, tailless, legless. Yellow-brown and black pattern resembles dead leaves. Flies direct, round wings often producing whistling sound. Voice: nasal **beep**; musical chippering of aerial song produced partly by wings! Prefers moist woodlands and wet thickets. Breeds locally almost throughtout; winters chiefly south of Delaware, Missouri.

Greater Yellowlegs

COMMON SNIPE (WILSON'S) A much more **slender, shapely, dark-backed** edition of woodcock preferring marshes, wet meadows, bogs. Back and crown striped, under parts whitish, smaller eyes in normal position. Flight starts off in zigzag course revealing pointed wings, rusty tail; bird usually uttering harsh **scape**. Voice: metallic, rail-like **kĭk-kĭk-kĭk**; rising and falling **zu-zu-zu-zu** of flight song produced by tail! Breeds south to n.w. Pennsylvania, Illinois, South Dakota; winters chiefly south of Delaware, s. Ohio Valley.

WHIMBREL (HUDSONIAN CURLEW). Only curlew with broad, dark stripes on crown; only species likely to be seen east of the Mississippi. Striking decurved bill usually 3-4 inches long. Often crow size; dusky-brown, paler beneath; no wing-stripe. Voice: rapid, staccato, whistled cook-cook-cook-cook; also sweet, tremulous notes. Prefers extensive mudflats or moist meadows. Breeds chiefly in Arctic; migrates mostly along coast; winters in South America, very few north to Florida.

UPLAND PLOVER (BARTRAM'S SANDPIPER). Not a plover. Larger than robin, slightly larger than killdeer with thin neck, small head, long tail, short, slender bill. Mostly mottled brown, paler beneath; no wing-stripe, no conspicuous marks. Prefers extensive fields of low grass; often perches on posts, momentarily elevating wings on alighting; often flies with rigid, downward tilted wings, vibrant wing-tips. Voice: rapid liquid kwĭp-ĭp-ĭp-ĭp, also weird, drawn-out, whistled way-leeeeeeee rising and falling, like sound of distant gale. Breeds from s. Quebec, Wisconsin south to Virginia, Oklahoma; winters in South America.

SPOTTED SANDPIPER. Only shorebird with large, dark, round spots on white breast. Smaller than robin; uniform olive-brown above, dark line through eye. Habitually teeters tail; flies with rigid, downward-tilted wings, quivering wing-tips. Fall and immature: no spots but easily identified by shape and actions as well as olive-brown back and white stripe over eye. Voice: high, clear, whistled pee-weet-weet-weet-weet. Widely distributed along coastal waters as well as inland ponds and streams. Breeds south to n. South Carolina, s. Louisiana; winters north along coast to South Carolina.

SOLITARY SANDPIPER. Slightly smaller than robin; slender, habitually nods head; usually found singly or in twos. Uniformly olive-brown above, white below; long, dark legs, white eye-ring. Graceful swallow-like flight, deep steady wing-strokes, lack of wing-stripe, barred white sides to tail conclusive. Voice: high, thin *peent*. Demands fresh water edges, occurring even along woodland pools and streams. Breeds south to northernmost U.S.; migrates throughout; winters in tropics.

WILLET. Only large, brownish-gray, thick-billed shore-bird with extensive black and white bands covering half of wing. Smaller than bantam hen. Larger, heavier than greater yellowlegs with long, dark legs, thick, dark bill. Vociferous: loud, whistled, oft-repeated *pill-will-willet*; rapid, sharp, *kip-kip-kip*. Prefers extensive mudflats, moist meadows. Breeds in Nova Scotia, along coast from New Jersey to Texas, on prairies from Iowa west; winters along coast north to North Carolina.

GREATER YELLOWLEGS. Slightly over 1 ft. in length. Slender, mostly gray above, white below. Long, bright-yellow legs; long, thin, very slightly upturned dark bill. In flight dark-gray above, no wing-stripe, in contrast whitish rump and tail. Vociferous: loud, arresting, whistled *you-you-you-you-you* (usually 3-5 notes); in spring mellow *whee-oodloo-oodloo-oodloo-oodloo*. Prefers mudflats, lake and river shores. Breeds in Canada; migrates throughout; winters along coast, most south of Virginia.

LESSER YELLOWLEGS. Small, slim edition of preceding (average 10 inches); bill straighter, shorter, distinctly thinner. Voice: softer, less forceful *you-you* (usually 1 or 2 notes). Breeds in Canada; migrates throughout East; winters chiefly south of U.S., few north of South Carolina.

KNOT. Only relatively short-billed shorebird with pale-red breast. Robin size, stocky, short-legged. Upper parts mostly gray and rufous, rump whitish. Fall and winter: silvery-gray above, white below, white stripe over eye. In flight, white wing-stripe, pale tail, whitish rump. Voice: low, whistled *flew-flew*. Prefers sandy flats. Breeds in Arctic; migrates chiefly along coast; winters mostly south of Georgia.

PURPLE SANDPIPER. Only sandpiper normally found in winter on Canadian and New England coasts. Usually confined to rocks. Smaller than robin; **chubby; mostly dark-gray with white belly, short yellow legs, slender, yellow-based slightly decurved bill.** In flight very dark with contrasting white wing-stripe. Voice: **twit-twit.** Breeds in Arctic; winters along coast south to New Jersey, rarely South Carolina.

PECTORAL SANDPIPER. Robin size; brown and heavily streaked above; dark crown; **brown upper-breast sharply defined against rest of white under parts; yellowish legs** (bird looks like large least sandpiper). Has relatively smaller head and longer neck than other sandpipers of its size. In flight identified by size; dark breast and rump; lack or virtual lack of wing-stripe. Voice: harsh **kreek.** Prefers grassy mudflats. Breeds in Arctic; winters in South America.

WHITE-RUMPED SANDPIPER. Only small native sandpiper with distinct white rump (conspicuous in flight). Smaller than robin, size of spotted sandpiper. Upper parts rusty-brown streaked with black; under parts white; breast washed with buff and distinctly streaked; legs dark; wing-stripe white. Fall: mostly pale-gray; rump, belly and stripe over eye white. (In any plumage separated from pectoral sandpiper by smaller size, white rump, dark legs, distinct wing-stripe.) Voice: sharp, abrupt **weet.** Prefers very wet mudflats. Breeds in Arctic; winters in s. South America.

LEAST SANDPIPER. Smallest shorebird, length of song sparrow. Upper parts, neck, breast mostly rich-brown; under parts white. (Separated from semipalmated sandpiper by **yellowish legs, browner back and crown, thinner bill.**) Voice: high **cree-eep.** Prefers grassy mudflats. Breeds in Canada; migrates throughout; winters along coast, chiefly south of Cape Hatteras.

DUNLIN (RED-BACKED SANDPIPER). Only sandpiper with black belly. Slightly smaller than robin; ruddy

above, whitish below; long, slightly decurved, dark bill. Fall
and immature: dingy-gray, paler below. **(Size, dingy color, decurved bill, dark legs identify it.)** In flight, white wing-stripe,
dark tail. Voice: nasal cheer and treep. Prefers grassy mudflats.
Breeds chiefly in Arctic; probably migrates throughout, seen
mostly around Great Lakes and along coast; winters along
coast, rarely north of New Jersey.

DOWITCHER. Only snipe-like bird with showy white
tail, rump and stripe up lower back. Slightly larger than robin,
brown above, rusty below; very long, straight, dark, snipe-like
bill. Fall and immature: dingy-gray; white stripe over eye. (Size;
long bill; white tail, rump and stripe on lower back conclusive.)
Voice: quick, sliding too-too-too. Prefers flooded mudflats in
open country; rapidly probes with long bill. Breeds mostly in
Arctic; migrates throughout, chiefly along coast; few winter
north of South Carolina.

SEMIPALMATED SANDPIPER. Our most abundant
shorebird. Sparrow size. (Almost identical to least sandpiper
but **chubbier, grayer with thicker, straighter bill, blackish
legs.)** Voice: sharp cri-ip. Prefers extensive sand and mudflats.
Breeds in Arctic; migrates throughout; winters along coast, seldom north of South Carolina.

MARBLED GODWIT. Only large, buffy-brown shorebird with very long, slightly upturned bill. Crow-size; long,
dark legs; basal half of bill flesh-colored; in flight uniformly
mottled brown (no white areas). Voice: harsh god-wit be-
quick. Breeds on inland prairies east to Minnesota; rare migrant
in East; winters locally along coast north to South Carolina.

SANDERLING. Small, chubby ocean beach sandpiper
habitually running in and out at edge of each wave. Smaller
than robin; mostly rusty-brown with whitish belly, black bill,
dusky primaries. Fall and winter: very white, slightly grayer
above, bill and legs black. In any plumage long, wide, white

Continued on page 121

Half mallard size.
Expert diver. Prefers
weedy pools and
marsh ponds. Only
grebe with thick bill.
(p. 40)

Pied-billed Grebe

Almost size of swan;
weight often 8 lbs.,
wing-spread 6½ ft.
Only dark pelican;
only one plunging
headlong into water
after fish.   *(p. 45)*

Brown Pelican

Smaller than Can-
ada goose, decided-
ly slimmer. It fre-
quently swims with
just head and neck
protruding above
the surface, thus
snake-bird. *(p. 49)*

Anhinga (Water-turkey)

Great Blue Heron

Often 4 ft. tall with 6-ft. wing-spread. Common, large, blue-gray heron, erroneously called crane by many. *(p. 51)*

Snowy Egret

Less than half the size of great blue heron. Only white heron with black legs plus golden slippers. *(p. 51)*

Green Heron

Only dark, stocky, crow-sized heron. Stretches its neck, raises crest and flicks tail when alarmed. *(p. 52)*

Only medium-sized blue-gray heron with black and white head. Yellow wash on crown seldom obvious. *(p. 53)*

Yellow-crowned Night Heron

Smallest heron; average length 1 foot. Confined chiefly to dense swamp vegetation; difficult to see or flush. *(p. 53)*

Least Bittern

Almost half the size of great blue heron. Spoon-shaped bill and pink plumage separate it from all other birds. *(p. 57)*

Roseate Spoonbill

99

Canada Goose

Our birds usually 7-14 lbs. in weight. Most common and widely distributed goose in East. Black head and neck with contrasting white chin-strap is conclusive. *(p. 59)*

Mallard Duck

Average length 2 ft., weight 2½ lbs. Only broad-billed duck with conspicuous white neckring separating green head and neck from rusty breast. *(p. 62)*

Blue-winged Teal

Half mallard size. Separated from green-winged teal in any plumage by large pale-blue patch on front of wing. *(p. 64)*

Smaller than mallard. Only duck with long, broad, spoon-shaped bill. Adult male with green head and chestnut sides unmistakable. *(p.64)*

Shoveler

Decidedly smaller than mallard. Male our most versi-colored iridescent duck. It prefers flooded woodlands, habitually perching in trees. *(p.64)*

Wood Duck

Smaller than mallard. One of our most abundant and widely distributed diving ducks. Generally occurs in large compact flocks. *(p.66)*

Scaup Duck (Blue-bill)

Almost eagle-sized carrion eater. Only vulture with long slim tail. It glides with uptilted wings, tipping from side to side as it scans the ground. *(p. 71)*

Turkey Vulture

Large and majestic hawk; wing-spread sometimes over 7 ft. Adult only eagle with snow-white head and tail. *(p. 77)*

Bald Eagle

Size of bantam hen. Confined to salt marshes along the coast. Almost identical to king rail but grayer. *(p. 86)*

Clapper Rail

Half mallard size. It prefers extensive and open marshlands. Only gallinule with bright-yellow legs or blue forehead shield. *(p. 87)*

Purple Gallinule

Half mallard size. Prefers weedy ponds and also marshland pools. When alarmed usually skitters and patters along surface into protection of dense vegetation. *(p. 88)*

American Coot

Smaller than robin. Prefers wide, sandy beaches. Separated from all similar-looking species by long, thick, black bill. *(p. 90)*

Thick-billed Plover (Wilson's)

Robin size. Prefers moist rocky shores and sandy beaches. Robust as a plover but thinner-billed, shorter-legged.

(p. 91)

Ruddy Turnstone

Smaller than a bantam hen. Only large brownish-gray thick-billed shorebird with extensive black and white bands covering half of wing.

(p. 94)

Willet

Size of robin. Prefers mud flats and marsh pools, lake and river shores. Breeds in Canada, known over most of U. S. only as a transient.

(p. 94)

Lesser Yellowlegs

Larger than herring gull. Dark-slate mantle distinctive. Found chiefly along the coast and on the Great Lakes *(p. 127)*

Great Black-backed Gull

Our most common and widely distributed gull. Average length 2ft., wing-spread 4²/₃ft. *(p. 126)*

Herring Gull

Smaller than herring gull. The black ring around the yellowish bill of adult conclusive. *(p. 127)*

Ring-billed Gull

Much smaller than herring gull. Chiefly coastal. Adult with its slate head, dark-gray mantle and its almost uniformly black wing-tips unmistakable. *(p. 127)*

Laughing Gull

Size of pigeon. Our most common and widely distributed tern. Black-tipped carmine bill identifies it. *(p. 130)*

Common Tern

Smaller than herring gull. In winter plumage quickly separated from Caspian tern by orange bill, white forehead. *(p. 131)*

Royal Tern

Crow length. Chiefly coastal. Our only bird whose lower mandible projects far beyond its upper one. *(p. 132)*

Black Skimmer

Size of pigeon. Our only bird with large triangular red, blue and yellow bill. Confined to coastal waters, chiefly from Maine northward. *(p. 134)*

Atlantic Puffin

Smaller and slimmer than our domestic pigeon, with longer pointed tail. Wings produce a whistling sound when bird flushes. *(p. 135)*

Mourning Dove

Size of robin. Our only small owl with "ears". Occurs in two color phases, gray or red-brown. *(p. 138)*

Screech Owl

Smaller than the robin. Breeds chiefly in Canada; known over most of eastern U.S. only as a winter visitor. *(p. 140)*

Saw-whet Owl

Robin size. In flight resembles the giant swallow with erratic bounding flight periodically punctuated by its quick-flitting wingbeats. *(p. 141)*

Common Nighthawk

Our very smallest eastern bird, weight equal to that of one penny. Generally seen hovering in front of flowers.   (*p. 143*)

Ruby-throated Hummingbird

Excluding virtually extinct ivory-bill, only crow-sized woodpecker, only one with crest. Rare to uncommon in most areas.   (*p. 146*)

Pileated Woodpecker

Robin size. Only ladder-backed woodpecker with red cap. Red wash on belly obvious on some males.   (*p. 146*)

Red-bellied Woodpecker

Red-headed Woodpecker

Robin size. Only woodpecker with entire head red, only one that habitually catches insects on the wing.   (*p. 146*)

Downy Woodpecker

Smaller than robin. A pocket edition of the hairy woodpecker but outer tail feathers show black barring.   (*p. 147*)

Eastern Kingbird

Robin size. Only flycatcher with broad white band on tip of tail.   (*p. 148*)

Song sparrow size; in flight appears larger. Our only swallow with pure white under parts. *(p. 153)*

Tree Swallow

Song sparrow size, chunky; it has least shape of any swallow. Only swallow with buffy rump, only one square-tailed in appearance. *(p. 153)*

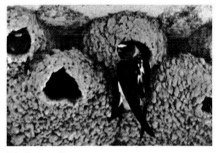

Cliff Swallow

Slightly larger than robin. Our only large bright-blue, white bird with a crest. *(p. 155)*

Blue Jay

Black-capped Chickadee

Smaller than song sparrow. Frequently seen hanging upside down or swinging like an acrobat from slender twigs.

(p. 158)

House Wren

Smaller than song sparrow. Grayest of wrens. Prefers to nest in bird houses, also in gardens and orchards. *(p. 162)*

Marsh Wren (Long-billed)

Smaller than song sparrow. Only wren with broad stripes on back. Prefers cattail marshes.

(p. 163)

Slightly larger than the robin, but more slender and long-tailed. Has habit of periodically elevating wings. *(p. 164)*

Mockingbird

Robin size. Our only uniformly dark and slate-gray bird with a black cap.
(p. 164)

Catbird

Larger than robin. Separated from the thrushes by long tail, long curved bill, white wing-bars, streaks rather than spots on breast, yellow instead of black eyes. *(p. 164)*

Brown Thrasher

Slightly smaller than robin. Only thrush with bright reddish-brown on head, neck and upper back.

(p. 166)

Wood Thrush

Much smaller than robin. Only bright-blue bird with a red breast.   *(p. 167)*

Common Bluebird

Robin size. Separated from great gray shrike by black of bill and feathers just above bill. *(p. 173)*

Loggerhead Shrike

Size of a robin but chunky and short-tailed. Appears all black at a distance. *(p. 173)*

Starling

Size of small song sparrow. Only vireo with blue-gray head and has conspicuous white spectacles. *(p. 176)*

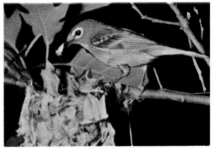

Solitary Vireo (Blue-headed)

Size of song sparrow. Only vireo with a distinct black bordered white stripe over eye. *(p. 176)*

Red-eyed Vireo

Very small, some only 4¼ inches long. Only bluish warbler with yellow throat and breast. *(p. 188)*

Parula Warbler

Smaller than song sparrow. Only warbler with broad white band across black tail. *(p. 184)*

Magnolia Warbler

Smaller than song sparrow. Only dark-looking warbler with both white throat and yellow rump.
(p. 186)

Myrtle Warbler

Smaller than song sparrow. Male only warbler with black hood that encloses bright yellow cheeks and forehead.

(p. 184)

Hooded Warbler (female)

Size of robin. Only black bird having bright yellow head. Occurs chiefly west of the Mississippi.

(p. 193)

Yellow-headed Blackbird

Foot-long iridescent black bird with long tail, graceful stride, pale-yellow eyes.

(p. 194)

Purple Grackle (Crow-Blackbird)

Brown-headed Cowbird

Smaller than robin. Male our only black bird with a brown head. *(p. 194)*

Scarlet Tanager

Larger and stockier than song sparrow. Male our only scarlet bird with black wings and tail.

(p. 196)

Cardinal

Size of small robin. Male our only red bird with a crest. *(p. 198)*

Size of small song sparrow with a short tail. In the summer adult male is mostly deep blue but appears black at any distance. *(p. 199)*

Indigo Bunting

Shorter and chubbier than the robin. Male is only yellow songbird with very large thick-based whitish bill. *(p. 199)*

Evening Grosbeak

Size of small song sparrow. Male only small bright yellow bird with black wings, tail and forehead. Often called wild canary. *(p. 201)*

American Goldfinch

119

Slightly smaller than robin. Prefers brushy thickets especially in the open woodlands. Habitually scratches among leaves.

(p. 202)

Eastern Towhee

Slightly larger than song sparrow Separated from white-crown by sharply defined white throat, flatter head, yellow between eye and dark bill. (p. 206)

White-throated Sparrow

Length 5–6³/₄ inches. Our most common and widely distributed sparrow. Prefers brushy thickets and shrubbery in gardens. (p. 208)

Song Sparrow

Continued from page 96

wing-stripe. Voice: snappy **quick-quick**. Breeds in Arctic; migrates chiefly along Great Lakes and coast; winters along coast, rarely north of New Jersey.

STILT FAMILY
Recurvirostridæ

Black-necked Stilt

THESE large, unique shorebirds are characterized by the extreme length of their slender legs, the extreme slenderness of their long, pointed bills.

BLACK-NECKED STILT. Only shorebird with amazingly long, slender, red legs. Length 14 inches; slender build; black above, white below; long, thin, black bill. In flight white tail and rump contrast with rest of solid black upper parts. Vociferous: wild, rapid **yip-yip-yip**. Prefers marshes. Breeds in Florida, coastal Louisiana, Texas, occasionally South Carolina; very few winter along coast of Louisiana, Texas.

121

PHALAROPE FAMILY
Phalaropodidæ

Northern Phalarope

PHALAROPES look like small, long-necked sandpipers with lobate feet. They are the smallest birds found swimming on the open ocean. They swim expertly, often spinning in circles and dipping their bills rapidly to pick up food. The females are more brightly colored than the males, make most of the advances in courtship, and leave all the cares of incubation and raising of young to their mates!

WILSON'S PHALAROPE. Only phalarope nesting in U.S., only one with no wing-stripe. Size of robin; slim, long-legged, long-necked, **needle-billed. Habitually runs rapidly in shallow water** or along shore pursuing tiny prey. Adult female: gray above, white below; wide black band from eye down neck, turning chestnut and extending onto back. Adult male: gray-brown above, white below, rusty wash on neck. Fall and immature: mostly white, grayer back **(identified by needle-bill, actions, shape).** In flight unstriped gray wings and back; white tail and rump. Voice: astonishingly deep **toot**; nasal **work**. Prefers fresh water marshes (rarely seen on the ocean). Breeds on prairie marshes southeast locally to Iowa, Indiana, rarely farther; rare migrant in East; winters in South America.

NORTHERN PHALAROPE. Locally common on open ocean, uncommon along shore, rare inland. Smaller than robin;

black needle-like bill. Female: gray-brown above, whitish below, rusty on side of neck, white throat. Male: duskier, less rusty on neck. Fall and immature: mostly gray above; striped back, whitish under parts, black eye-stripe, black, needle-like bill. In flight conspicuous white wing-stripe, dark tail. Voice: sharp **wit-wit.** Breeds in Arctic; migrates chiefly off shore; winters on South Atlantic.

RED PHALAROPE. In breeding plumage only phalarope with dark-red under parts. Slightly larger than preceding; uniformly dark-looking except for white cheeks, white wing-stripe. Fall and immature: mostly white; grayer on back, black eye-patch, yellow base to bill; in flight white wing-stripe. (Separated from northern by chubbier build, paler, unstreaked back, **whitish crown, thicker yellow-based bill).** Voice: sharp **wit-wit.** Breeds in Arctic; migrates chiefly across ocean, rare even along shore; winters on South Atlantic.

JAEGERS
Stercorariidæ

THESE Arctic breeders migrate off our coast but since they seldom come near the shore one must ordinarily go out on the open ocean to study them. They impress one as gulls with hawk-like mannerisms. In fact their bills are hooked, their webbed feet sharply clawed, their flight as dashing, agile and swift as that of a falcon. They habitually pursue gulls and terns, following every twist and turn until the victim in desperation drops its fish. They occur in two phases, one dark all over, the other mostly dark above, white beneath. Most show a white flash at the base of the primaries. The adults have the two central tail feathers projecting beyond the rest of the tail. Mottled immature jaegers without elongated tail feathers can be separated only by experts.

POMARINE JAEGER. Largest jaeger, some size of herring gull. **Central tail feathers broad and twisted, usually appearing as single, wide three-inch blade.** White at base of primaries very conspicuous.

Parasitic Jaeger

PARASITIC JAEGER. Most common. Smaller, slimmer; thinner-billed than preceding. Wings more slender and angled, less white at base of primaries. **Two central tail feathers project as separate points,** often as much as four inches.

LONG-TAILED JAEGER. Very rare. Most delicate and graceful of jaegers; half weight of pomarine. Unlike preceding species light-phased adults have no breast-band. Pointed central tail feathers stream three to six inches or more behind. White at base of primaries often inconspicuous.

GULLS
Larinæ

Herring Gull

WHEREAS gulls are more abundant over the sea or along the coast, many occur on the Great Lakes, several like the herring, ring-billed, and Bonaparte's frequent smaller bodies of water, while the Franklin's gull occurs chiefly in the interior and is rare along both east and west coasts. Thus the general usage of 'sea gull' is misleading and should be avoided. Some are as small as a domestic pigeon, others as large as a small goose but they are all robust and in the adult plumage mostly pearl-gray and white. The name long-winged swimmers is descriptive. They swim buoyantly with tail held off the water. In flight they usually carry their thick, slightly hooked bills horizontally. Their long, narrow, pointed wings enable them to fly, soar and glide with a grace surpassed by few birds. As a rule the smaller the gull the quicker the wing-beats, the smallest species almost tern-like in actions. Although they occasionally make shallow dives they are essentially scavengers, picking food from the surface with their bills. They frequently perch on buoys, posts, breakwaters and boats as well as on land where they walk quickly and easily. They are gregarious often occurring in flocks of several hundred or more. The term 'mantle' frequently used in describing gulls and terns, signifies the upper surface of the wings and the portion of the back between them.

I have seen observers confuse gulls with shearwaters, gannets, jaegers, terns and ospreys. Shearwaters have narrower tails, hold their wings more rigidly extended, and begin each long twisting glide with a few very rapid wing-beats. The gannet with its large size, long heavy pointed bill, long pointed tail and spectacular dives should cause no trouble. Jaegers have sharply hooked bills, more angled wings and a dashing hawk-like flight. Most of our terns are smaller and daintier with deeply forked tails. All of them have sharply pointed bills which they generally carry tilted downward instead of straight out. While fishing they take headfirst plunges from the air. The broad angled wings and jagged rounded wing-tips of the osprey are enough to distinguish it from any gull.

HERRING GULL. Our most common and widely distributed gull. Average length 2 ft.; wing-spread 4 2/3 ft.; weight 2½ lbs. White body, pearl-gray mantle, black wing-tips spotted with white, **flesh-colored legs,** yellow bill. Immature: dusky-brown; dark bill, tail and eye (with age birds progressively change to adult plumage). Voice: loud **kak-kak-kak;** wild squalling **yuk-yuk-yuk-yukkle-yukkle-yukkle;** loud **kee-ow.** Widely distributed; breeds south to Great Lakes and Long Island; winters throughout.

GLAUCOUS GULL. Unlike most gulls this and the Iceland have **no black on wing-tips.** Glaucous slightly larger than herring gull, often size of great black-back. Mostly white with pale grayish-white mantle, white wing-tips. Immature: first winter; creamy-white, white wing-tips. Second winter; uniformly snow-white. Voice: deep throaty **kuk-kuk-kuk;** wailing kä-yukkä yukkä yukkä. Breeds in Arctic; rare winter visitor to Great Lakes and along coast to Delaware, casually farther.

ICELAND GULL. Almost identical to glaucous gull but usually smaller (herring gull size), bill shorter and slimmer; adults' eye-ring red, not yellow. A race called Kumlien's has gray spots on wing-tips. Large Iceland gulls are the size of small glaucous gulls; these borderline birds must be identified with great caution. Voice: very similar to herring gull's; staccato kak-kak-kak; loud kee-ak; wailing yak-yakka yakka yakka yakka. Breeds in Arctic; rare winter visitor to Great Lakes and along coast to Delaware, casually farther.

GREAT BLACK-BACKED GULL. Larger than herring gull; length 2½ ft., wing-spread 5½ ft. White body, dark-slate mantle, black wing-tips spotted with white, flesh-colored legs, heavy yellow bill. Immature: head, body, base of tail gray-white, contrasting with dark back which with age changes from golden-brown to dark-slate. Voice: deep guttural kuk-kuk-kuk; harsh deep bark aou. Breeds south to Coastal New England; winters on Great Lakes, more commonly along coast south to North Carolina, occasionally Florida.

RING-BILLED GULL. Almost identical to herring gull but smaller (length 1½ ft.; wing-spread 4 ft.); legs green-yellow, bill yellow ringed with black, wing-tips mostly black. Immature: similar to corresponding stages of herring gull (even legs and bill usually flesh-pink) but terminal tail-band narrower; smaller size obvious when comparison is possible. Voice: softer, higher-pitched than herring gull's. Breeds south to Lake Ontario; winters almost throughout eastern U.S., most in southern states.

LAUGHING GULL. Much smaller than herring gull. Length 1 1/3 ft.; wing-spread 3 ft. Body white, head deep-slate, mantle dark-gray, wing-tips black, bill and legs dark-red. Winter adult: dark smudges on whitish head. Immature: small, dark with white rump and belly. Voice: mirthful staccato kă-hă; loud laughing nasal ăyăă ă hă-hă-hă ăăă ăăă. Coastal; breeds north to Nova Scotia; winters chiefly south of Charleston.

FRANKLIN'S GULL. Very similar to preceding; slightly smaller, mantle paler, conspicuous white areas separating mantle and black wing-tips. Winter adult: loses black head but has dark band on back of head from eye to eye. Immature: very similar to corresponding stages of laughing gull, only to be identified by experts. Voice: soft, plaintive poor-lee. Breeds on prairie marshes east to Minnesota; formerly rare migrant east of the Mississippi, now becoming regular to Lake Erie in autumn.

BONAPARTE'S GULL. Half size of herring gull, almost tern-like. Length 13 in., wing-spread 32 in. Mostly white; head sooty, mantle pearl-gray; long white patch on front edge of wing, black edge around tip of wing, legs orange, bill black. Winter adult: loses black head but has black spot behind eye. Immature: gray-brown band across wing from elbow to back; narrow black band on tail, black spot on cheek. Usually silent, occasionally a nasal, shrill peer. Breeds in northern Canada; migrates throughout; winters chiefly along southern coasts, some on Great Lakes and on saline waters north to New England.

BLACK-LEGGED KITTIWAKE. Small oceanic gull, so pelagic that outside the breeding season it seldom is seen from shore. Looks like very small herring gull (length only 1½ ft.) but has black legs and feet (not flesh-colored), almost solid black wing-tips. Immature: tail tipped with black, often slightly notched; black band on back of neck, black spot behind eye; black of wing-tips extends up front edges of wings to elbows, then diagonally to middle of back forming large black V on each wing. Voice: nasal get-a-way or kitt-i-wake. Breeds along ocean south to Gulf of St. Lawrence; winters on north Atlantic, seldom south of Delaware; accidental inland.

TERNS
Sterninæ

Common Tern

MOST of our terns look like small streamlined gulls but they have more slender, sharply pointed bills, longer, deeply forked tails and longer, narrower, more pointed wings. In the air they are even more graceful, with a bounding flight and a swift dashing manouverability reminiscent of swallows. Unlike gulls, they frequently fly with their bills pointed down toward the water. They often hover to get the range before plunging headfirst after tiny fish. Terns infrequently swim, preferring to ride some floating driftwood or settle along the shore. They can walk with surprising grace even though they have tiny feet, and legs so short that their bodies nearly touch the ground. Most of them are pearly-gray above, white beneath, black-capped (in the fall this cap receeds to expose a white forehead). Like gulls they frequently occur in tremendous flocks but they are much more migratory, relatively few spending the winter north of Georgia.

COMMON TERN. Our most common and widely distributed tern. Pigeon size but slimmer; tail deeply forked. Mostly white with black cap, pearl-gray mantle, **dusky wing-tips,** white tail, carmine feet, **black-tipped carmine bill.** Winter: bill darker, forehead and crown white; black patch around back of head. Voice: harsh downward slurred **tee-arrr;** short **kik-kik-kik.** Breeds mostly along coast and around Great Lakes; some winter in Florida.

FORSTER'S TERN. Almost identical except for **black-tipped dull-orange bill, whitish wing-tips.** Winter: **separate black patch on each side of head** across eye and ear. Voice: sharp, nasal **zzeap.** Breeds in coastal marshes north to Maryland, in western inland marshes northeast to Illinois; winters along coast south of Virginia.

ARCTIC TERN. Almost identical to common tern but **bill usually smaller and blood-red to tip,** body and face grayer, tail slightly longer. Fall birds with dark bills seldom can be distinguished from common and roseate terns in the field. Voice: similar to common tern's; only high-pitched whistled **kee-kee** and harsh **teee-yä** distinctive. Strictly maritime. Breeds along coast south to Massachusetts; migrates at sea, accidental in U.S. south of breeding grounds.

ROSEATE TERN. Almost identical to common tern but **bill usually mostly black,** tail longer, mantle paler, especially primaries. (At rest tail extends well beyond wing-tips, common tern's tail barely reaches wing-tips.) Immature and fall adult: rarely separable in the field from common and Arctic terns. Voice: harsh **crack;** distinctive soft musical **cheery.** Breeds locally along coast from Nova Scotia to Texas; winters south of our borders.

LEAST TERN. Quite similar to preceding terns but smaller (robin size) with white forehead, black line through eye, yellow feet, black-tipped yellow bill. Voice: quick musical **klee-dee**; sharp, high **kik-kik.** Breeds along coast to Massachusetts and up the Mississippi to Iowa; few winter in Florida and on Gulf coast.

ROYAL TERN. Very similar to more widely distributed Caspian tern but slightly smaller, more fork to tail, **more orange bill,** black cap with **shaggy crest. Winter: shaggy black crest behind white forehead.** (Caspian tern has grayish streaked forehead, practically no crest, harsher calls.) Voice: short shrill **keer.** Strictly coastal, breeds north to Virginia; winters chiefly south of Charleston.

CASPIAN TERN. Our largest tern, **almost herring gull size.** Mostly white; pearly-gray mantle, dusky wing-tips, slightly crested black cap, large **red bill. Winter:** similar but **grayish streaked forehead.** Voice: loud harsh **kaarrr.** Breeds locally along Gulf coast, on Great Lakes and Gulf of St. Lawrence; winters chiefly south of Charleston.

BLACK TERN. Only robin-sized black tern; wings gray. **Winter:** whitish beneath; black blotches on white head. Voice: sharp **klee-ä** and **kik-kik.** Breeds on inland marshes south to w. Tennessee, northeast to c. New York, rarely farther. Widely distributed on migrations; winters in South America.

SKIMMERS
Rynchopidæ

THERE are three species in this unique family. Their amazing bills are long, compressed laterally, almost blade-like, the lower mandibles projecting forward nearly one-fourth farther than the upper ones. At rest the birds look like crow-lengthed elongated terns with legs so short their bodies barely clear the ground. I never have seen one rest on the water, but I would be surprised if they could not do so. Ordinarily they gather in compact flocks on sand bars or mud flats. In flight

Black Skimmer

their exceptionally long narrow wings carry them with great buoyancy. They skim close to the water, their blade-like bills often cutting the surface as in long lines, V-formations or compact flocks they play follow-the-leader. Skimmers are very noisy, baying a soft nasal yăp-yăp. They occur chiefly in coastal bays and estuaries, but outside North American some are found regularly on large rivers far from the ocean.

BLACK SKIMMER. Our only bird with lower mandible projecting far beyond upper one. Bird jet-black above, white beneath; amazing black-tipped red bill. Immature: browner with duller, more even bill. Breeds along coast from Texas to New York, occasionally farther; winters mostly south of Cape Hatteras.

AUKS
Alcidæ

Razor-bill

THE members of this family are our only penguin-like birds. They are chubby, walk upright and are mostly black and white. They are essentially maritime, swimming buoyantly on the wildest seas with head pulled close to the body. They dive from the surface, traveling expertly beneath the water, using both their webbed feet and wings for propulsion. In the air they look like small, fast, chunky, short-necked ducks with very rapid-moving, narrow wings. They generally fly close to the water and perch chiefly on bold ocean rocks. They breed in colonies on northern islands, some guillemots and a few puffins as far south as Maine. In the eastern United States they are known primarily as off-shore winter visitors to New England.

RAZOR-BILL (RAZOR-BILLED AUK). Only auk with high narrow razor-bill. Smaller than mallard, size of small duck. Heaviest of family with thick neck, large head;

while swimming **habitually cocks tail upright.** All of head and most of upper parts black; under parts white; white stripe across black bill. Winter and immature: lower face, throat and sides of neck white; immature's bill much smaller. Voice: human-like groans and grunts. Breeds on coastal islands south to Bay of Fundy; winters on Atlantic to Massachusetts, few to Long Island, casually farther.

DOVEKIE. Our only robin-sized auk; only one with very short bill. Black above, white beneath, black bill. Wingbeats rapid, almost bumblebee-like. Breeds in Arctic; winters on Atlantic. Periodically driven ashore by wild easterly storms, sometimes as far south as Florida!

BLACK GUILLEMOT. Our only Alcid (Auk Family) with large white shoulder-patches. Pigeon size. Mostly sootyblack; thin, pointed black bill, orange-red feet. Winter adults and immatures: mostly grayish-white, distinct white shoulderpatches on gray wings. Wing-beats rapid almost bumblebee-like. **Habit of nervously dipping bill in water diagnostic.** Voice: high thin whistle. Breeds as far south as Maine coast, yet in winter accidental south of Massachusetts.

ATLANTIC PUFFIN. Our only bird with huge triangular red, blue and yellow bill. Pigeon size; very chunky. Black above, white beneath, sides of face pale-gray. In winter: bill smaller and dull-colored, cheeks dusky. Voice: deep nasal **hey-al;** various groans. Breeds as far south as Matinicus Rock, Maine, yet accidental in winter south of that state.

PIGEONS
Columbidæ

ANYONE who knows the common domestic pigeon found in city parks will recognize all of our native pigeons and doves as close relatives. They are plump-bodied birds

134

with small heads and slender bills. They spend a great deal of time on the ground, usually jerking or nodding their heads as they walk. All are exceptionally fast fliers with powerful wing-beats. Their cooing is characteristic.

Mourning Dove

ROCK DOVE (DOMESTIC PIGEON). Average length 13 inches. This well-known introduced bird has become self-sustaining in many areas and deserves a place on our bird list as much as the pheasant, starling and house sparrow.

MOURNING DOVE. The common wild pigeon of the East. Smaller and slimmer than domestic pigeon with longer pointed tail. Mostly brown; white spots around rim of tail. Wings produce whistling sound when bird flushes. During winter travels in flocks. Voice: mournful hollow coo-ăh-oo ooo ooo ooo. Prefers farmlands. Breeds almost throughout; most move to southern states for winter.

GROUND DOVE. Almost as small as song sparrow. Mostly gray with dark, square tail. Usually on ground, nods head as it walks. In flight flashes rufous on wings. Voice: soft repetitious coo-oo. Resident of low coastal country from South Carolina to Texas.

135

CUCKOOS
Cuculinæ

Yellow-billed Cuckoo

THESE slow deliberate birds are longer, much slimmer and more graceful than robins. They are usually very secretive, slipping noiselessly through the leafy thickets they prefer to haunt. They have thin slightly decurved bills and long, slim, rounded tails. Our species are mostly brown above and white beneath. Although ordinarily very quiet and difficult to find, they periodically break forth with loud cuckoo calls that carry long distances. Many of the coo calls are so similar that it is often impossible to say which species is singing; some however are distinctive. Our only bird that remotely resembles a cuckoo is the brown thrasher, but it is much heavier and thicker-billed with conspicuous white wing-bars and heavily streaked breast.

YELLOW-BILLED CUCKOO. Only cuckoo with rusty on wings. Slightly longer than robin; yellow base to bill, large white spots on black tail feathers. Voice: distinctive throaty kà-kà-kà-kà-cow cow cow cowlp cowlp cowlp; numerous repetitious liquid or gutteral coo calls, many inseparable from similar calls of black-bill. Prefers moist thickets. Breeds virtually throughout, more commonly in southern half of U.S.; winters in South America.

BLACK-BILLED CUCKOO. Similar but no rusty on wings, bill black, only small spots on tips of brown tail feathers; adult's eye-ring red. Voice: distinctive rapid rhythmic kuk-kuk-kuk kuk-kuk-kuk kuk-kuk-kuk. Prefers tangles of second growth. Breeds south to North Carolina and Arkansas; winters in South America.

OWLS   *Tytonidæ* and *Strigidæ*

Screech Owl

THESE fluffy soft-plumaged birds of prey have their exceptionally large eyes fixed firmly in sockets in the front of the face, forcing them to turn their large rounded heads in the direction they wish to look. This in conjunction with their round or heart-shaped flat faces gives them a human appear-

137

ance. They are rather shapeless, neckless and broad-headed. They possess sharp hooked bills and powerful talons to aid them in capturing and devouring their prey. Although most are nocturnal, they can see in the daytime, some even hunting then. Their flight is soft and noiseless, some like the short-eared and barn owl's bounding and wavering, others like the horned and burrowing owl's swift and direct. Goatsuckers with their fluffy brown plumage and somewhat owlish faces may confuse beginners. These birds however, never have hooked bills or sharp talons, they perch in a horizontal position instead of up-right, and have medium-sized eyes on the sides of a rounded face instead of very large eyes in front of a flat face.

SPECIES WITH CONSPICUOUS EAR-TUFTS

SCREECH OWL. Our only small owl with 'ears'. Size of robin, mostly gray or red-brown, eyes yellow. Voice: mournful quavering tremulo usually running down scale oo-oo-oo-oo-oo (easily imitated by tilting head back and whistling through saliva gathered on fore part of tongue). Common around villages and farms. Resident almost throughout.

HORNED OWL (GREAT HORNED). Powerful looking; larger, stockier than crow, often 2 ft. long. Mostly dark-brown with numerous black bars, conspicuous white throat, yellow eyes, ear-tufts wide apart. Voice: deep hoo hoo-hoo hoo hoo; blood-curdling shrieks. (Barred owl's hoots baritone, not bass; usually eight hoots in two groups of four.) Prefers woodlands. Resident throughout.

LONG-EARED OWL. Smaller than crow. Mostly dark-brown, eyes yellow. Usually elongates itself to look very slender. (Differs from horned owl in smaller size, ear-tufts close to-gether, lengthwise streaking beneath.) Voice: low soft whoop whoop whoop; numerous wildcat calls. Prefers
138

woodlands. In winter often occurs in small flocks. Breeds south to Virginia and Texas; winters throughout.

SPECIES WITHOUT CONSPICUOUS EAR-TUFTS

BARN OWL. Only owl with heart-shaped whitish monkey-face. Crow size. Tawny back, whitish under parts, dark eyes, very long legs. In flight looks all white from below. Voice: harsh explosive hissing kschhh. Prefers farmlands and villages. Habitually lives in church belfrys, silos, haylofts, deserted buildings. Resident north to Massachusetts, Michigan, Nebraska.

SNOWY OWL. Only white owl. Larger, stockier than crow; average length 2 ft. Sometimes barred with black or brown; eyes yellow. Diurnal (active during day). Voice: loud barking krow-ou. Rare winter visitor to open country in northern states.

BURROWING OWL. Brown, robin-sized, terrestrial owl with yellow eyes and rather long legs. Quite diurnal; bounces when nervous and bobs head. Voice: liquid quick-quick-quick; mournful coo-oo. Confined to prairies of s. Florida and West.

BARRED OWL. Appears larger, much broader than crow. Mostly gray-brown; **large puffy barred collar, dark eyes.** Voice: eight hoots in two groups of four, ending drawled: who cooks for you? who cooks for you-all? Often heard during day. Prefers moist woodlands. Resident throughout.

SHORT-EARED OWL. Tiny 'ears' seldom visible. Smaller than crow, **streaked buffy-brown,** eyes yellow. Terrestrial, preferring extensive marshlands. Frequently hunts in daytime; in winter occurs in small flocks. Voice: rasping mammal-like kee-yow!; rapid toot toot toot. . . . Breeds south to New Jersey, Ohio, Kansas; winters throughout.

SAW-WHET OWL. Smaller than robin. Back cinnamon-brown spotted with white, under parts white streaked with brown; crown streaked, eyes yellow, bill black. Voice: mechanical repetitious whistled **tu tu tu tu.** . . . Breeds chiefly in Canada and northernmost U.S.; winters south to North Carolina and Louisiana.

GOATSUCKERS
Caprimulgidæ

Common Nighthawk

To MOST people these birds are only voices in the dark. All except the nighthawk are strictly nocturnal, and at most seasons even this bird does not begin its activities until twilight. In the daytime they usually are found resting on the ground or lengthwise along some limb, their tiny feet seldom visible. They are mostly robin size, have soft mottled brown plumage, and owlish faces with large dark eyes on the sides of the head. They have a noiseless bounding flight, often gliding, floating, twisting as they go. They feed on the wing, their enormous mouths enabling them to catch insects with ease. At rest the long pointed wings of the nighthawk reach the end of the forked tail, while in the others the longer rounded tail projects well beyond the rounded wing-tips.

WHIP-POOR-WILL. Robin size, mostly mottled brown with black throat. Male: white on sides of tail and under black throat. Voice: loud, quick, emphatic, repetitious whistled whip-poor-will. Prefers woodlands near extensive fields. Breeds south to Virginia, Alabama, n.e. Texas; some winter along coast north to South Carolina.

CHUCK-WILL'S-WIDOW. Larger, buffier with brown throat. Voice: slow, oft-repeated whistled chuck-will's wid-ow. Prefers low country woodlands (often erroneously called whip-poor-will). Breeds north to Maryland, Ohio and Kansas; some winter in Florida.

COMMON NIGHTHAWK. Robin size. Mottled gray-brown; white patch across wing. Male: white patch across forked tail and on throat. Most active at dusk; sometimes diurnal, especially during migrations. In flight resembles giant swallow with erratic bounding flight periodically punctuated by quick-flitting wing-beats. (In the evening pairs of terns often indulge in queer ceremonial flights with stiff uptilted quick-flitting wing-beats. If seen in silhouette at such times they look surprisingly nighthawk-like.) Voice: nasal peent, also booming sound at end of courtship dives. Prefers open country; some nest on city roofs. Breeds locally throughout; winters in South America.

SWIFTS
Apodidæ

Chimney Swift

THERE are great size, color and tail differences in swifts, but they are all immediately recognizable as members of this interesting family. Our sooty-black chimney swift, the only swift in the East, is the size of a small song sparrow but due to the length of its wings appears much larger in flight. Overhead it looks almost head-less and tail-less. This in conjunction with its long narrow slightly curved wings has given the bird the two popular names: 'bow and arrow bird' and 'cigar with wings'. In flight the long paddle-like wings usually are fully extended, never deeply folded like those of swallows; they give the false impression of beating alternately as the bird tips from side to side on its rapid gliding and quivering erratic dash across the sky. This flight is entirely different from the graceful buoyant movement of swallows. In the evening swifts may appear bat-like but the broad rounded wings and bounding flapping flight of the small mammals set them apart. The rapid chippering notes of chimney swifts are distinctive. These birds rarely perch except in chimneys, hollow trees and occasionally deserted buildings. They breed almost all over the eastern United States and southern Canada and winter in South America.

HUMMINGBIRDS
Trochilidæ

Ruby-throated Hummingbird

THE SMALLEST needle-billed hummingbirds are the tiniest feathered creatures in the world. Usually they are associated with flowers. Most are so small and insect-like that they sometimes are confused with sphinx moths by inexperienced observers. Their wing-beats are so fast (50-75 times a second) that the wings appear as hazy as an airplane propeller in motion. The birds generally are seen buzzing and hovering before flowers, moving either forward, backward, upward or downward with equal ease. When perched most of them appear thumb-sized or smaller, their long needle-like bills conclusive.

RUBY-THROATED HUMMINGBIRD. Only species found over most of the East. Our smallest eastern bird: length 3-3¾ in.; weight equal to that of one penny. Mostly green above, white below. Male: dark throat glows ruby-red in some

143

lights. Female: white throat, white spots on tip of tail. Breeds throughout; winters in tropics, few north to s. Florida.

KINGFISHERS   *Alcedinidæ*

Belted Kingfisher

THE kingfishers make up a large diversified family. There is no reason here to analyze the taxanomic characteristics common to them all. Our belted kingfisher, the only species occurring in the East is unmistakable. It is larger and bulkier than a robin with a long strong bill, short tail, and a large disheveled crest which makes it look exceptionally big-headed. The male is mostly gray-blue above, white beneath with a conspicuous gray-blue breast-band. The female has an additional rusty breast-band and a rusty wash on the sides. This bird's bluish caste and crested head give it only a superficial resemblance to the more streamlined, long-tailed, neatly-creasted, brighter-colored blue jay. The kingfisher frequently is seen perching patiently on some dead branch or wire near the water, or hovering in one spot above the surface, getting ready for the headfirst plunge after fish. Its vigorous rattling notes can be heard easily a quarter of a mile away. This species breeds in sandy banks throughout the East, but most individuals move to the southern states for winter.

WOODPECKERS
Picidæ

Hairy Woodpecker

WOODPECKERS are highly specialized for perpendicular climbing. Their feet with two sharp toes in front and two behind firmly cling to the wood while their stiff pointed tail feathers press firmly against the trunk as a prop. Ordinarily they are seen exploring trunks and branches, climbing jerkily with head well back and alert expression. All are built sturdily and have strong chisel-like bills for digging out grubs. They drum their songs with the mechanical rhythm of a welding machine. Due to their manner of flight, several quick wing-beats and a pause, they rhythmically dip up and down. Although nuthatches habitually climb perpendicular trunks and branches and hack away at them, they should cause no confusion. Nuthatches are smaller and more compact with stubby tails which are never braced against the tree for support. They walk rather than climb and regularly move headfirst down a trunk, a feat no woodpecker could perform.

YELLOW-SHAFTED FLICKER. Only eastern woodpecker with brown back, only one commonly feeding on ground. Larger than robin, mostly yellow-brown; red patch on back of head, black spots on breast, black crescent across chest. In flight flashes yellow under wings and tail, shows conspicuous white rump. Male: black whiskers. Voice: loud kee-you; rhythmic wick-up wick-up; repetitious yuck-yuck-yuck . . . . Breeds throughout; most leave northern states in winter.

PILEATED WOODPECKER. Only crow-sized woodpecker, only one with crest (except nearly extinct ivory-bill). Mostly black, conspicuous red crest; white throat, white stripes on sides of neck and wings, dark bill. Voice: whistled yuk-yuk-yuk more musical than flicker's; loud cook cook cook cook cook. Usually rare to uncommon local resident in woodlands throughout.

RED-BELLIED WOODPECKER. Only ladder-backed woodpecker with red cap. Robin size. Under parts mostly buffy-white, red wash on belly obvious on some males. Immature: crown and nape gray. Voice: noisy; harsh cha-chack. Resident north to Delaware, Lake Erie, s. Minnesota.

RED-HEADED WOODPECKER. Only woodpecker with entire head red, only one that habitually catches insects on the wing. Robin size. White under parts, rump and wing-patches; black back, shoulders, wing-tips and tail. Immature: head gray-brown. Voice: high-pitched tchur. Local resident north to New York, Michigan, Minnesota (absent from large areas).

YELLOW-BELLIED SAPSUCKER. Only woodpecker with longitudinal white stripe on upper part of closed wing. Smaller than robin. Mostly black and white; yellowish under parts, red forehead, red throat on male. Immature: browner, wing-stripe distinctive. Voice: squealing cat-like way. Breeds south to New England, Indiana, Missouri, in mountains to North Carolina; winters chiefly in southern states.

HAIRY WOODPECKER. This and next our only white-backed woodpeckers. Robin size. Under parts white, rest spotted and checkered with black and white. Bill long. Male: red patch on back of head. Voice: metallic **keek**; kingfisher-like rattle. Resident in woodlands throughout.

DOWNY WOODPECKER. Pocket edition of hairy woodpecker but outer tail feathers show black barring. Short bill and weak, high pitched notes best means of separation. Resident throughout.

RED-COCKADED WOODPECKER. Only ladderbacked woodpecker with white cheeks. Almost robin size. Black cap, nape and middle tail feathers; mostly white under parts; black wings spotted with white. Male: small red spot on either side of crown. Voice: harsh **shritt**. Resident in open pine forests north to Virginia, Kentucky, Missouri.

FLYCATCHERS
Tyrannidæ

FLYCATCHERS are surprisingly sedentary for birds and their manner of feeding is characteristic. They perch upright and motionless on an exposed branch, post or wire, periodically fly out to snatch some passing insect and immediately return to one of their favorite perches to patiently await the next victim. They range from sparrow to robin size, have flat broad bills, short legs and small weak feet. Waxwings, starlings and some warblers periodically dart forth to catch insects on the wing, but none of our flycatchers is as chunky and black as a starling, none as trim and sharply crested as a waxwing, none as small and dainty as the flycatching warblers.

Great Crested Flycatcher

EASTERN KINGBIRD. Only flycatcher with broad white band on tip of tail. Robin size. Slate above, white beneath. Often flies with stiff quivering wings held below horizontal. Voice: shrill staccato **tsee-tsee.** Prefers farmlands, frequently perching on posts and wires. Breeds throughout winters in tropics.

GRAY KINGBIRD. Resembles eastern kingbird but slightly larger, much paler gray above, much larger bill, no white on pale notched tail (eastern kingbird has dark rounded tail with broad white terminal band). Voice: sputtering peter-hurry. Prefers mangroves or coastal meadows stippled with small trees. Breeds along Florida coasts, few to Georgia; winters in West Indies.

GREAT CRESTED FLYCATCHER. Only eastern flycatcher with cinnamon tail. Robin size. Mostly brown above with cinnamon in wings; gray breast, yellow belly. Very noisy: loud whistled wheep wheep and rolling prrru distinctive. Prefers woodlands. Breeds throughout, some winter north to Florida.

EASTERN PHOEBE. No other flycatcher wags tail so regularly and emphatically. Smaller than robin. Mostly gray-brown above, gray-white below. (Unlike wood pewee no wing-bars, no yellow on bill.) Distinctly says pheebee! Prefers proximity of cliffs, bridges or farm buildings. Breeds south to Texas and mountains of Georgia; winters in southern states.

EASTERN WOOD PEWEE. Quite similar to phoebe but slightly smaller, does not wag shorter tail; has two whitish wing-bars, yellow on lower mandible. Plaintive, slurred, whistled pee-a-wee conclusive. Prefers woods. Breeds almost throughout; winters in tropics.

OLIVE-SIDED FLYCATCHER. Large-headed, short-tailed almost robin-sized flycatcher. Our only flycatcher with dark flanks contrasting with otherwise whitish under parts. Usually seen on tip-top of tallest tree. Mostly dark olive-brown above; white tufts often showing between wings and lower back. Voice: loud whistled hic three-beers; repetitious trebled pep-pep-pep. Prefers conifers especially in slash areas or flooded woodlands. Breeds south to Minnesota, Massachusetts, in mountains to North Carolina; winters in South America.

SPARROW-SIZED flycatchers with conspicuous eye-rings and prominent wing-bars. They have mostly olive-brown upper parts; the whitish under parts are washed with gray, buff or yellow. All very similar, best told by call and habitat.

YELLOW-BELLIED FLYCATCHER. Under parts and eye-rings often yellow enough to be conclusive. Prefers moist conifer woodlands. Whistles abrupt **perwee.** Breeds south to northernmost U.S.; winters in Central America.

ACADIAN FLYCATCHER. Prefers moist deciduous woodlands. Sneezes **ka-zeek.** Breeds north to New York and s. Michigan; winters in South America.

ALDER FLYCATCHER (TRAILL'S). Prefers wet willow and alder thickets. Says **phebeeo** or **witch-brew.** Breeds south to New Jersey, West Virginia, Arkansas; winters in Central America.

LEAST FLYCATCHER. Less particular, almost any scattering of trees will do. Snaps **chebéck!** Breeds south to New Jersey, Oklahoma, in mountains to North Carolina; winters in Central America.

LARKS
Alaudidæ

THE horned lark is our only representative of the true larks. The tiny 'horns' are not always visible. Unlike the great majority of small birds it usually walks and runs, seldom hops. It is slightly larger than a song sparrow, mostly brownish above, gray-white beneath. It has a black patch under the white or yellowish throat, one on each side of the face, the male another across the fore part of the crown. Between breed-

Horned Lark

ing seasons horned larks normally travel in flocks. They are essentially terrestrial, preferring expanses of open barren country with a scattering of short grass. Their call note is a high-pitched **tsee-tsee**; their song, a delicate high musical twittering, often is delivered high above the ground as the bird flutters on quivering wings. Horned larks are widely distributed. They breed locally south to North Carolina, Missouri and coastal Texas; winter almost throughout the states, the population at this season being greatly augmented by more yellow-faced birds which breed in Canada. Our American meadowlarks belong to the blackbird family and are discussed with that group.

SWALLOWS
Hirundinidæ

SWALLOWS are built essentially for a life in the air and usually are seen flying gracefully and effortlessly with strong wing-beats around farmlands or over fields, marshes and ponds, snatching insects as they go. Their light airy flight is characterized by brief periods of floating, frequent shifts in direction and abrupt changes in speed. They are gregarious and

Barn Swallow

most frequently perch on wires or dead branches, sitting with erect posture almost shoulder to shoulder. Then one notices the wide flat mouths, long slender wings and small weak feet. All of our species except the cliff swallow have noticeably forked tails. Most are sparrow size but due to the length of their wings appear much larger in flight. Chimney swifts erroneously called chimney swallows by many people are in a different family. They appear almost tailless, hold their wings much more rigid, and have an unmistakable quivering erratic flight.

TREE SWALLOW. Our only swallow with pure white under parts. Song sparrow size. Metallic blue-green or brown above. Voice: sweet musical cheep and chee-weep. Nests in hollow trees or bird boxes. Breeds south to Virginia and Kansas; winters along coast, chiefly south of Virginia.

BANK SWALLOW. Smallest swallow (length 5-5½ inches), only one with distinct dark band across breast. (Juvenile tree swallow often has faint narrow breast-band.) Brown above, white beneath. Voice: soft abrupt ffrrutt. Nests in large compact colonies, stippling perpendicular sandy banks with holes. Breeds south to Virginia and Texas; winters in South America.

ROUGH-WINGED SWALLOW. Only brown-backed swallow with dusky throat. Larger, browner than bank swallow, no breast-band. Voice: unmusical burp-burp. Nests singly or in small loose groups in holes in banks, bridges, dams, etc. Breeds north to Massachusetts and Minnesota; winters in Central America.

BARN SWALLOW. Only swallow with deeply forked tail, only one with very slender needle-like points to wings and tail. Slightly larger than song sparrow, very slim. Dark steel-blue above, salmon to buffy-white beneath, rusty forehead, white hemstitching on tail. Juveniles have shorter outer tail feathers. Voice: sweet twittering sweeter-sweet sweeter-sweet; soft twit-twit. Constructs open-topped mud nests in buildings, under porches, rarely under rock ledges. Breeds south to North Carolina and Arkansas (locally to Gulf); winters mostly in tropics.

CLIFF SWALLOW. Only swallow with buffy rump, only one appearing square-tailed. Song sparrow size. Chunky, least shape of any swallow. Dark-blue back, dusky under parts, chestnut throat, buffy forehead. Voice: nasal cat-like yaa. Globular mud nests with entrance at sides placed under eaves and on cliffs, usually in compact colonies. Breeds south to Alabama and Texas; winters in South America.

PURPLE MARTIN. Only large dark swallow. Largest swallow, some robin size. Male: uniformly blue-black. Female: browner with light belly. Voice: rich whistled **tu-tu**; warbly **tu-tu-tu tu tu-weedle**. Nests in colonies in hole-filled trees, more often in many-roomed bird houses. Breeds locally throughout East; winters chiefly in Brazil.

JAYS
Garrulinæ

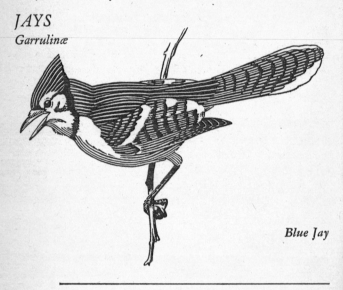

Blue Jay

THE DASHING, alert, handsome jays are slightly larger than a robin with longer, broader, more fan-shaped tails. Ordinarily they are bold, inquisitive and noisy with a decided ability for creating excitement. However they can be extremely quiet and secretive, especially during the breeding season. Although related to the crows they do not walk but move about with long graceful hops. Most of them are brightly colored, all have strong broad bills and short rounded wings. When not nesting they usually travel in small flocks, preferring the protective cover of woods, shaded gardens and brushy thickets.

GRAY JAY (CANADA). Only jay mostly gray, only one with white forehead. Black patch on back of white head, black stripe through eye. Juvenile: darker gray, even on head. Voice: harsh chă-chă-chă; metallic squeaks and squawks; soft ka-whee-ah. Resident in conifer or mixed woodlands, south to northernmost states.

BLUE JAY. Our only large bright-blue and white bird with a crest; only eastern jay with crest. Mostly blue-gray above; bright-blue on wings and tail, whitish beneath, black rim around white face and throat. Voice: loud, scolding, cat-like jay jay jay; musical whistled plinky-plinky; numerous squawks and whistles; perfect imitation of red-shouldered hawk's kee-you. Common and widely distributed resident in woodlands of East, even on shaded city streets.

SCRUB JAY (FLORIDA). Our only crestless blue jay. Wings, tail and most of head solid blue (no white spots), back brownish, under parts dirty-white. Voice: variety of harsh squawks. Found only in scrublands of Florida peninsula; subspecies common in West.

CROWS
Corvinæ

ALMOST everybody recognizes the large, conspicuous, noisy, glossy-black crows. They are much larger and more robust than any of the true blackbirds and have decidedly larger, stronger bills. They are powerful, confident, alert and difficult to approach. Their loud caws are among the most widely known sounds in nature. Except during the breeding season they travel in flocks, some winter roosts often exceeding ten thousand birds. Whereas they spend much time in the protection of the woodlands they feed chiefly on the ground, expertly walking around in fields and pastures.

COMMON CROW. The common crow over most of the East. Large (17-21 inches long), chunky, glossy-black. Voice: loud **caw-caw-caw** well known. Resident almost throughout, but most birds from Canada and northernmost U.S. move south for the winter.

Common Crow

FISH CROW. Slightly smaller, safely identified only by distinctive calls: a hoarse *crăăă-crăăă* and a staccato ca-a. These two characteristic calls are decidedly different from the caws of young crows. Found mostly along the coast as far inland as tide penetrates. Breeds north to s. New England; winters chiefly in the South.

COMMON RAVEN. Larger than crow with longer tail, heavier bill, shaggy throat. Sails and soars more expertly, revealing longer, wedge-shaped tail, longer, thicker neck;

more horizontal wing position (crow sails less expertly, holding wings tilted upward). In warm weather the raven invariably flies with its bill wide open. Voice: deep **crrruck**; loud weird drawn out **crrräää**; high **tŏc-tŏc-tŏc**. Resident in wild country south to Maine, Michigan, Minnesota, in mountains to Georgia.

TITMICE
Paridæ

Black-capped Chickadee

THESE small, plump, mostly grayish bundles of vitality are the gymnasts of our woodlands. They usually are seen hopping actively from limb to limb, frequently hanging upside down or swinging like acrobats from slender twigs, as they industriously search for insects. Their long, slender, soft tails are never used as props. They are smaller than most sparrows with a plumage that looks especially soft and fluffy. Their large heads have big beady inquisitive eyes and small pointed bills. Their cheerfulness and friendliness make them the favorites of many people, particularly in winter when they travel in small flocks, frequent window feeding shelves and even land on familiar hands and shoulders to beg for food. They readily respond to whistled imitations of their simple calls.

157

BLACK-CAPPED CHICKADEE. Smaller than song sparrow. Black cap and bib, white cheeks, gray back, whitish under parts, brown wash to sides. Voice: distinctly says chicka-dee-dee-dee; whistles a clear pee-beee. Resident south to New Jersey, Ohio, Missouri and in mountains to North Carolina.

CAROLINA CHICKADEE. Almost identical. Slightly smaller, less white on edges of wing feathers. Safely separated from black-cap only by notes and range. Voice: chicka-dee-dee-dee higher, more hurried; whistled pee-bee pee-bee. Common chickadee of the South, resident north to range of preceding.

BROWN-CAPPED CHICKADEE (BOREAL). Almost identical to preceding chickadees but distinctly browner, cap dark-brown, notes slower, more nasal and wheezy; chee chee zay zay. Resident in conifer woodlands south to northern parts of Maine, New York, Michigan and Minnesota.

TUFTED TITMOUSE. Our only small smooth-gray bird with distinct crest. Song sparrow size. Sides of whitish under parts washed with brown. Voice: lively whistled peter peter peter; scolding nasal ya-ya-ya. Resident north to New Jersey, Lake Erie, Iowa.

NUTHATCHES
Sittidæ

ANY SMALL, stout, compact bird walking head-first down a perpendicular tree trunk as easily as it walks up is a nuthatch. They are sparrow size or smaller, have strong straight sharply-pointed bills, and stubby tails which never are braced against the tree for support.

Due to their trunk and branch explorations, beginners might confuse them with woodpeckers, but woodpeckers never move headfirst down a perpendicular surface, they are larger, they climb rather than walk, and in climbing their longer tails always are pressed against the tree for support.

White-breasted Nuthatch

WHITE-BREASTED NUTHATCH. Only black-capped nuthatch with clear white cheeks. Largest species, song sparrow size. Bluish-gray above, white beneath; conspicuous black beady eye; chestnut under tail-coverts seldom visible. Voice: grunts a nasal yank-yank; in spring, low whistled rapid ya-ya-ya-ya-ya. Resident almost throughout, common in many areas.

RED-BREASTED NUTHATCH. Only nuthatch with black line through eye. Much smaller than song sparrow. Black cap, gray-blue back, rusty wash to whitish under parts. Voice: toots a high-pitched nasal yaa-yaa. Prefers conifers. Breeds south to northernmost states, in mountains to North Carolina; known in most eastern states only as transient or winter visitor.

BROWN-HEADED NUTHATCH. Only nuthatch with **brown cap** (this cap extends to eye). Our smallest nuthatch, some only 4 inches long. Blue-gray above, white beneath. Voice: rapid, high-pitched, often incessant **yip-yip-yip.** Resident in southern pinelands north to Delaware, Missouri.

CREEPERS
Certhiidæ

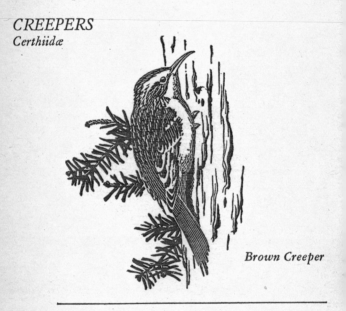

Brown Creeper

No ONE can mistake the brown creeper the only North American representative of this large diversified family. It is our only very small extremely slim brown bird that creeps mouse-like up the perpendicular trunk of a tree. It is smaller and much slimmer than a song sparrow. It is mostly brown above and gray-white below with a long slender decurved bill, and a long stiff tail which is firmly pressed against the bark for support. It frequently creeps in a spiral up one tree industriously searching for food and after reaching a good altitude drops to the base of the next tree to resume the seemingly endless task. Although ordinarily solitary, loose flocks of a dozen or more may be encountered during migrations. The usual note of the creeper is a thin prolonged **tseeee**. On the breeding grounds it delivers a long delicate high-pitched **see-see-see-tweesee**. In the East the brown creeper breeds chiefly in Canada and the northernmost states and is known in most areas only as a winter visitor.

WRENS
Troglodytidæ

Marsh Wren

THESE small, plump, mostly brown bundles of energy frequently keep their tails cocked over their backs. Most are smaller than sparrows with short, rounded wings and thin, pointed bills. They are so active, perky, bustling—even impertinent—that they often will approach an intruder, scolding him harshly. Inexperienced observers could confuse them with sparrows but sparrows do not have such thin bills, short upcocked tails or vivacious manners and actions.

NO DISTINCT WHITE LINE OVER EYE

HOUSE WREN. Grayest of wrens, lacks distinct markings. Smaller than song sparrow. Gray-brown above, pale-gray beneath. Voice: loud gurgling warble; harsh scolding cha-cha-cha. Prefers gardens and orchards. Breeds south to Virginia and Missouri; winters in southern states.

WINTER WREN. Only wren with dark under parts and dark barred belly. Mostly dark-brown; pale almost imperceptible line over eye. One of our smallest birds; almost round with absurdly short upright tail. Voice: indescribable flow of delicate trills and warbles; sharp kip-kip. Prefers brush piles, slash areas, thickets in wooded ravines. Breeds south to northernmost states, in mountains to Georgia; known only as transient or winter visitor in most of East.

SEDGE WREN (SHORT-BILLED MARSH WREN). Only wren with streaked crown but streaks being delicate are usually impossible to see in the field. One of our smallest birds, some only 4 inches long. Secretive, difficult to study. Mostly brown upper parts, brown-washed under parts, fine streaks on back, faint buffy eye-stripe. Quickly separated from marsh wren by lack of conspicuous white eye-stripe or by dry unmusical song: chip-chip-chip-chip-chip-chirrrrrrrrr. Prefers wet meadows. Breeds from s. Maine and Manitoba to Delaware, e. Kansas; winters chiefly south of breeding range.

DISTINCT WHITE LINE OVER EYE

CAROLINA WREN. Our largest and rustiest wren (song sparrow size). Rusty above, buffy wash below, conspicuous white stripe over eye. Voice: clear lively whistled **tea-kettle tea-kettle tea-kettle,** or **wheedle-wheedle-wheedle.** Prefers dense tangles of vines and bushes. Resident north to New Jersey, Ohio, s. Iowa, occasionally farther.

BEWICK'S WREN. Only wren with mostly whitish under parts, only one with white outer-tips to tail. Some song sparrow size. Very slim. Mostly brown above, white stripe over eye. Tail which it nervously flirts from side to side is long, often fanned, revealing white corners. Voice: sweet song quite similar to, but more delicate than song sparrow's. Prefers gardens, and thickets in open country. Resident in interior south of s. Michigan; rare on Atlantic coast and in northern tier of states.

MARSH WREN (LONG-BILLED MARSH WREN). Only wren with broad stripes on back. Smaller than song sparrow. Conspicuous white stripe over eye, solid brown crown, mostly brown upper parts, whitish buff-washed under parts. (Quickly separated from sedge wren by distinct white eye-stripe or gurgling liquid warble; from Carolina wren by small size, stripes on back, song, and usually habitat). Prefers cat-tail marshes. Breeds north to Maine and Saskatchewan; winters chiefly in southern states.

MOCKINGBIRDS
Mimidæ

ALL OF our representatives of this family are robin size or slightly larger, but most are proportionately slimmer and have more slender slightly decurved bills. Their longer tails are nervously pumped and switched back and forth whenever the birds are excited. Their strong legs are built for much ground work since they pass a great deal of time scratching among the leaves. They show a marked preference for brushy thickets and tangles of vines. All are superb songsters, generally selecting some high perch from which to demonstrate their vocal powers.

Mockingbird

MOCKINGBIRD. Slightly longer than robin, more slender and long-tailed. Has habit of periodically elevating wings. Mostly pale-gray and white; in flight conspicuous white patches on wings and tail (shrikes are stockier, shorter-tailed; have hooked bills, much black on wings, tail and mask). Voice: harsh tchack; enthusiastic variety of beautiful oft-repeated whistled notes and phrases interspersed with imitations and harsh calls. Resident north to Maryland, Illinois, Nebraska.

CATBIRD. Our only uniformly dark slate-gray bird with black cap. Robin size. Chestnut under tail-coverts seldom noticeable. A restless busybody. Voice: soft plaintive cat-like maaa; variety of sweet whistles and chuckles (seldom repeated in succession) interrupted by cat-like complaints. Breeds almost throughout; winters in southern states.

BROWN THRASHER. Larger than robin. Mostly rufous-brown above; white under parts heavily streaked with

164

brown. (Separated from thrushes by long tail, long curved bill, wing-bars, streaks rather than spots on breast, yellow instead of black eyes. Cuckoos are slimmer, slower, more deliberate, never have wing-bars or streaked breasts.) Voice: harsh smack; variety of paired or tripled sweet whistled notes and phrases .... you-you listen-listen I am here I am here, etc. Breeds almost throughout; winters in southern states.

THRUSHES
Turdidæ

Hermit Thrush

ALMOST everyone knows a robin. Forget the colors and just visualize the shape and actions of the bird, and one will have a mental picture of all our thrushes except the bluebird. They pass a great deal of time feeding on the ground, head often cocked to one side as though detecting some insect sound or movement. They stand erect, breast out, head high, and after a few quick steps or hops again pause with the same upright military posture. When alarmed they fly to some perch and instantly snap to attention with breast out, head high, wings smartly at sides. When relaxed the wings sometimes droop. They are all medium-sized birds (6½-10½ inches) with large dark eyes, moderately long slender bills, and legs well built for much ground work. They are among our best songsters.

I have known beginners to identify brown thrashers, fox sparrows and ovenbirds as thrushes. The thrasher is much larger and longer-tailed with longer bill, conspicuous white wing-bars, yellow instead of dark eyes, streaks instead of spots on its breast. The fox sparrow has none of the dignified posture and mannerisms of a thrush. It has a conical bill and streaks not spots beneath. The ovenbird is smaller and slimmer with a streaked instead of spotted breast, and an unthrush-like deliberate dainty-stepping walk.

ROBIN. Our largest thrush, only one with rufous breast. Length 8½-10½ inches. When excited flirts tail and flicks wings. Dark-gray back, darker head. Young have spotted breasts. Voice: lively cheerful whistled **cheer-up cheerily cheer-up cheerily cheerily**; scolding **wheep-wheep.** Prefers lawns, gardens, farmlands. Breeds south to n. Florida and Louisiana; winters chiefly in southern states.

WOOD THRUSH. Only thrush with **bright reddish-brown on head, neck and upper back.** Rest of upper parts duller brown; **many large conspicuous dark spots on white breast** and sides. Slightly smaller than robin, decidedly plump. Voice: beautiful, widely spaced flute-like phrases **ee-o-lay ah-lo-lea**; rapid liquid **pit-pit.** Prefers moist deciduous woodlands. Breeds from n. Florida north to c. New Hampshire, c. Minnesota; some winter in Florida.

HERMIT THRUSH. Only thrush with rusty tail. Tail briefly raised when bird is alarmed. Smaller than robin. Back brown, buffy-white breast heavily spotted. Voice: beautiful whistled phrases, rising and falling, each phrase introduced by a sustained note; low **chuck**; cat-like **tway.** Prefers mixture of evergreens and deciduous trees. Breeds south to Long Island, n. Michigan, c. Minnesota, in mountains to Virginia; winters chiefly in southern states.

SWAINSON'S THRUSH (OLIVE-BACKED). This and gray-cheeked only thrushes with dull olive-brown backs. Both smaller than robin with dusky-white under parts distinctly spotted high on buffy breast. Swainson's identified by **buffy cheeks and conspicuous pale-buff eye-ring.** Voice: repetition of eight to ten liquid pipe-organ notes spiraling upward; liquid quit; cat-like tweeur. Prefers conifer woodlands. Breeds south to n. New England, n. Michigan, in mountains to West Virginia; winters in tropics.

GRAY-CHEEKED THRUSH. Very similar to preceding, separated from it by **grayish cheeks, virtual absence of eye-ring.** Autumn birds of these two species often inseparable in the field. Voice: nasal hear; slurred veer vee-ur vee-ur veer veer (like veery's but weak and often rising at end). Prefers conifers. Breeds chiefly in Canada; a small race (Bicknell's) south to mountains of Massachusetts and New York; winters in South America.

VEERY. Only thrush with uniform **cinnamon-brown upper parts.** Smaller, slimmer than robin; only faint spots high on breast of whitish under parts. Voice: delicate downward slurred unforgettable veer vee-ur vee-ur vee-ur vee-ur; hummed-whistled view. Prefers moist woodlands with rich undergrowth. Breeds south to New Jersey, Ohio, Iowa, in mountains to Georgia; winters in South America.

COMMON BLUEBIRD. Only **bright-blue bird with red breast.** Female: paler. Young: mostly gray above, whitish below (little blue or red); breast speckled. Small, dumpy and gentle for a thrush. Habitually perches on posts and wires, dropping to ground only long enough to snatch food. Voice: soft, gentle, warbled purity. Prefers farmlands. Breeds almost throughout; winters chiefly south of New Jersey and Ohio.

GNATCATCHERS
Polioptilinæ

Blue-gray Gnatcatcher

IF ONE sees a tiny extremely slender bird with a long thin bill, and a long loose-hinged tail which it waves and cocks at an angle, nervously fluttering, hovering and flycatching among the branches it is a gnatcatcher. Our only birds with which they could be confused are the small active wood warblers, but none of these latter birds is so slender and none has such a long thin switching tail.

BLUE-GRAY GNATCATCHER. Our only representative. Much smaller and decidedly thinner than a song sparrow. Mostly blue-gray above, white beneath; white eye-ring, white-sided black tail. Voice: sharp **speeng**; high wiry **chee zee zee**. Prefers woodlands. Breeds north to southern parts of New Jersey, Michigan, Iowa; winters along coast north to South Carolina.

KINGLETS
Regulinæ

THESE are our only tiny, plump, almost round birds which habitually hang like acrobats from the tips of branches and nervously flirt their wing-tips as they move. They are among our smallest birds, averaging only four inches in length. They have very small bills, short tails and a soft, fluffy plumage that is mostly olive-gray above and whitish beneath.

Golden-crowned Kinglet

They are extremely active and restless, feeding chiefly at the tips of branches where they often flutter hummingbird-like in the air as they pick off insects. They are essentially arboreal showing a marked preference for conifers. Kinglets most closely resemble wood warblers but they are smaller, rounder, thinner-billed, shorter-tailed and ordinarily move their wing-tips more nervously.

GOLDEN-CROWNED KINGLET. Only kinglet with white stripe over eye, only one giving thin high lisping tsee-tsee-tsee. All except young birds show black-bordered yellow or orange crown. Mostly olive-gray above, yellow wash to wings and tail, whitish beneath. Voice: on breeding ground, series of thin ascending notes with descending chatter at end—**high high higher higher highest chatter.** Breeds chiefly in conifers south to Maine, Minnesota and in mountains to North Carolina; known over most of eastern states only as winter visitor.

RUBY-CROWNED KINGLET. Only kinglet with eye-ring, only one with harsh scold note. Upper parts olive-gray, under parts washed with buffy. Male often reveals ruby crown. Large black eyes are emphasized by the pale eye-ring, giving the bird a staring expression. Voice: astonishingly loud whistled see-see-see you-you-you just-look-at-me just-look-at-me just-look-at-me. Breeds in conifers south to northernmost states; winters chiefly in southern states.

PIPITS
Motacillidæ

Water Pipit

PIPITS are sparrow-like birds with very slender bodies, thin bills and long slender wagging tails. Unlike most sparrows they walk and run instead of hopping. They are strictly terrestrial, preferring great stretches of open treeless country, especially newly plowed fields, tidal marshes and cultivated lowlands. Outside of the breeding season they ordinarily travel in flocks, their light undulating flight distinctive.

WATER PIPIT (AMERICAN). Only eastern pipit. Uniform gray-brown upper parts; lightly streaked buffy under parts; white outer tail feathers, dark legs and bill. (Vesper sparrow has thick bill, white under parts, chestnut shoulders; does not wag tail, hops instead of walking.) Voice: thin pee-peet. Breeds chiefly in Arctic; winters mostly from Delaware and Ohio south to Gulf states.

WAXWINGS
Bombycillidæ

Cedar Waxwing

THESE gentle, conspicuously crested birds are smaller than a robin and decidedly slimmer. One immediately is impressed with their upright dignified posture, and their soft sleek gray-brown plumage which generally has every feather not only neatly in place but in superb condition. They have a yellow band on the tip of the short tail and red waxlike formations on the secondaries. The forehead, chin and line through the eye are velvety black. The dark bill is short and broad. Outside the breeding season they usually travel in large flocks. Waxwings frequently are seen picking berries, sometimes graciously passing a delicious morsel to another waxwing nearby! At times they dart out flycatcher-like to snatch insects on the wing.

CEDAR WAXWING. Only waxwing usually seen in the East, only one with white under tail coverts and definite yellow wash on belly. Juvenile grayer, distinctly streaked. Voice: high thin pssit. Prefers orchards. Breeds south to Georgia and Kansas; winters chiefly in southern states.

GREATER WAXWING (BOHEMIAN). Quite similar to preceding but slightly larger and grayer with chestnut instead of white under tail-coverts, two white patches in wing. (Cedar waxwings sometimes show white edges to wing-feathers and are mistaken for this northwestern bird.) The chestnut under tail-coverts, smooth-gray breast and more rattling notes are the best field marks of the greater. Voice: louder more rattling trrrr. Accidental in East. Breeds in w. Canada; irregular winter visitor to Minnesota, Wisconsin, casually farther south and east.

SHRIKES
Laniidæ

Loggerhead Shrike

SHRIKES are our only hawk-like song birds. They are the size of a robin with heavy heads, stout hooked bills, short legs and slim tails. Our species are gray, white and black with conspicuous black masks. Ordinarily they select a commanding perch and patiently wait to pounce upon insect, small rodent or bird. Because of their habit of impaling their prey on thorns and sharp branches they are widely known as butcher-birds. Shrikes prefer open country stippled with bushes. Their flight is direct, their wing-beats very rapid and in repeated series. They generally fly close to the ground ending each dash with a decided upward sweep to some prominent perch.

Since the mockingbird has a rather similar shape and gray and white plumage, it could cause momentary confusion, but the mocker is slimmer, longer-tailed and does not have a black mask or hooked bill.

LOGGERHEAD SHRIKE. Chiefly pale-gray above, white beneath; wings, mask and most of tail black. Bill and feathers just above bill black. Juvenile: pale-gray under parts faintly barred. Voice: harsh grating repetitious stop-and-see; also shack shack. Breeds locally almost throughout; winters chiefly in southern states.

GREAT GRAY SHRIKE (NORTHERN). Slightly larger than preceding. Breast finely barred, in winter often noticeably so. Feathers just above base of bill whitish (not black as in loggerhead). Flesh-colored base to lower mandible (except in late spring and summer). Immature: brownish; under parts distinctly barred, bill brown. Breeds in Canada; winter visitor to northern states, rarely south to Virginia, Kentucky, Texas.

STARLING
Sturnidæ

THESE immigrants from Europe are chunky and meadowlark-like in size and shape with equally short square tails. Though glossed with purple and green and sprinkled with dots they look all black at a distance. In spring and early summer their long slender bills are bright-yellow. Autumn and winter birds are dark-billed and heavily spotted with white.

Starling

Young birds are dusky-gray. Starlings feed mostly on the ground, their bustling waddling gait and short tails quickly separating them from blackbirds. They are gregarious except during the breeding season. In some cities winter roosts contain many thousands of birds. In flight their short tails and pointed wings give them a broad triangular shape. They travel with speed alternately flapping and sailing. Flocks wheel, glide and rush along in unison as though controlled by one master mind. They prefer cities, villages and farmyards, feeding chiefly on lawns, pastures and plowed fields. They frequently are seen whistling, sputtering and chattering from poles, wires and roof tops. The starling now occurs over most of our region and is steadily increasing in numbers and extending its range.

VIREOS
Vireonidæ

Red-eyed Vireo

VIREOS are small birds with olive-green backs and chiefly whitish or yellowish-white under parts. Most are song sparrow size or smaller. They resemble warblers but they are much slower and more deliberate and their thicker bills are slightly hooked at the tip. Ordinarily instead of flitting or rushing after insects as most warblers do, vireos carefully and methodically search twigs and leaves, turning their heads slowly, eyeing thoroughly every inch of vegetation. This leisurely inspecting head motion is diagnostic. Because they are unhurried and ordinarily well concealed by leaves, they are more often heard than seen. Most are tree dwellers, some prefer thickets but all hang their cup-like nests underneath the fork of a horizontal branch. In our representatives, all those having wing-bars also have eye-rings, those without wing-bars have eye-brow stripes.

SPECIES WITH WING-BARS AND EYE-RINGS

WHITE-EYED VIREO. Only white-throated vireo with yellow spectacles. Smaller than song sparrow. Mostly olive-green above, whitish below, white wing-bars, white eyes, yel-

lowish wash to sides. Voice: snappy **chicka-we-see-you** . . . . . .
chick; numerous chucks and warbles. Prefers thickets' of bushes
and vines. Breeds north to Massachusetts, Ohio, Wisconsin; some
winter along coast north to South Carolina.

BELL'S VIREO. Like white-eyed vireo but **paler, no yellow in spectacles, dark eyes, pale wing-bars.** Voice: hurried
cheedle-cheedle-chee? cheedle-cheedle-chew. Prefers thickets
by streams. Breeds chiefly west of the Mississippi, some northeast to Indiana; winters in tropics.

YELLOW-THROATED VIREO. Only vireo with
bright-yellow throat and breast. Size of small song sparrow.
Mostly olive-green above, white belly, yellow spectacles, white
wing-bars. Voice: slow rich hummed-whistled phrases **see-me
. . . . I am here . . . . how are you?** Prefers tree tops. Breeds
locally almost throughout; winters from Mexico southward.

SOLITARY VIREO (BLUE-HEADED). Only vireo
with **blue-gray head and conspicuous white spectacles.** Size
of small song sparrow. Mostly olive-green above, whitish below,
white throat, yellowish sides. Voice: like a sweet high-pitched
red-eye but more inflections, a frequently inserted rising **toweeto** conclusive. Prefers mixed woodlands. Breeds south to Minnesota, Michigan, Connecticut, in mountains to Georgia; some
winter in southern coastal states.

SPECIES WITHOUT WING-BARS
BUT WITH EYE-BROW STRIPES

RED-EYED VIREO. Only vireo with **distinct black-
bordered white stripe over eye.** Size of song sparrow. Mostly
olive-green above, white below; sides tinged with dusky-yellow,
gray crown. Voice: series of two to four note robin-like phrases
delivered deliberately, leisurely, incessantly; nasal mewing way.
Prefers deciduous woodlands. Our most common and widely

distributed vireo. Breeds almost throughout; winters in South America.

PHILADELPHIA VIREO. Only vireo without wing-bars having mostly yellowish under parts. Smaller than song sparrow. Chiefly olive-green above, pale eye-brow stripe. (Some orange-crowned and Tennessee warblers look quite similar but they are slimmer, have thin bills and quick active restless warbler actions.) Voice: similar to red-eye's but slower, more broken and higher-pitched. Prefers moist thickets. Breeds south to northern parts of New England, Michigan and Minnesota; winters in Central America.

WARBLING VIREO. Palest of vireos. Size of small song sparrow. Mostly grayish upper parts, whitish under parts, inconspicuous eye-brow stripe. Voice: hurried unbroken melodious warble rising at end (reminiscent of purple finch). Prefers tall shade trees. Breeds south to North Carolina, Louisiana; winters in tropics.

WOOD WARBLERS
Parulidæ

Black-throated Green Warbler

ALTHOUGH most of our warblers average between 5-5½ inches in length, they offer us a great deal of variety ranging in size from the 4¼ inch parula to the 7½ inch chat.

Almost all of them are smaller, more slender and more delicate than sparrows with thin pointed bills, and plumage gayly decorated with variegated colors. Usually they are active, quick, alert, almost tireless, some like the redstart habitually flitting flycatcher-like to snatch insects on the wing. They are essentially insectivorous, industriously, almost incessantly searching every leaf, twig and branch for food. The great majority are arboreal but some like the yellowthroat spend the major part of their lives in low dense tangles while a few like the ovenbird do practically all of their feeding on the ground. Most of them are known to us only as transients or summer residents, but a few spend the winter, chiefly in the southern states. In most forested areas they are common and widely distributed. In fact, in some northern woodlands more than half the birds present in summer are warblers.

Occasionally beginners confuse them with vireos and kinglets. Vireos have thicker, slightly hooked bills and are much more slow and deliberate. Kinglets are smaller, rounder, thinner-billed, shorter-tailed and ordinarily flirt their wing-tips more constantly and nervously.

In the following list I have omitted a few rare or extremely local warblers which most people are unlikely to encounter. It should be emphasized that the plumages of many immatures and autumn adults often are puzzling even to experienced students, and identification of these must be left to the experts.

NO CONSPICUOUS PATCHES OR BARS ON WINGS
DISTINCT STREAKING UNDERNEATH

YELLOW WARBLER. Our only very small bird that looks uniformly bright-yellow. Often called wild canary. Fine red streaks on breast distinct only in male; inconspicuous yellow wing-bars. Autumn birds duller. **In any plumage yellow tail-spots conclusive.** Voice: cheerful **sweet sweet sweet sweeter-than-sweet;** also **wheechee weechee wee.** Prefers small bushes especially in moist meadows. Breeds south to Missouri, n. Georgia; winters in tropics.

PALM WARBLER. Terrestrial habits and constant wagging of tail up and down very helpful. (Prairie only other warbler habitually wagging tail; waterthrushes teeter.) Upper parts olive, under parts mostly yellow, sides streaked with red, crown chestnut. Belly and eye-stripe white in western palm,

Ovenbird

yellow in yellow palm. Fall and winter: dingier, little chestnut on crown. Voice: weak, rapid, warbled tsee tsee tsee tsee. Breeds in conifer bogs south to Maine, Minnesota; common transient throughout; winters chiefly in southern states.

OVENBIRD. Only warbler that looks like a miniature thrush. Feeds mostly on ground, mincing dainty walk distinctive. Upper parts mostly brown-olive, under parts whitish heavily streaked with black, crown rufous bordered with black, white eye-ring emphasizes big eye. Voice: loud, emphatic, staccato teacher teacher teacher teacher teacher or teach teach teach teach usually increasing in volume. Prefers deciduous

179

woods. Breeds south to Arkansas, n. Georgia; few winter north to Florida, Louisiana.

NORTHERN WATERTHRUSH. This and next only warblers that teeter. They are large for warblers and usually are seen walking on moist ground along the water's edge. Back uniformly olive-brown, distinct pale-yellow eye-stripe; under parts yellowish heavily streaked with black (even on throat). Voice: loud, liquid, musical warble sweet-sweet-sweet ché-ché-ché chew-chew-chew; metallic pink. Prefers wooded swamps. Breeds south to n. Minnesota, New York, in mountains to West Virginia; few winter north to Florida.

LOUISIANA WATERTHRUSH. Slightly larger than preceding. Under parts mostly white and heavily streaked, eye-stripe distinctly white, throat unstreaked except for dark line on either side. Voice: wilder, more ringing than preceding, ending in confused mixture of chippering notes; metallic pink. Prefers brushy edges of woodland streams. Breeds from c. New England, Minnesota south to n. Georgia, n.e. Texas; few winter north to Florida.

CANADA WARBLER. Only warbler with uniformly smooth-gray upper parts. Mostly bright-yellow below; yellow spectacles. Male: necklace of black streaks. Practically no necklace on female, fall male or immature. Voice: jumpy emphatic sweet tea-cher-wip tea-cher-wip tea-cher-wip-wip. Prefers undergrowth in rich mixed woodlands. Breeds south to New Jersey, Minnesota, in mountains to Georgia; winters in South America.

NO CONSPICUOUS PATCHES OR BARS ON WINGS
NO DISTINCT STREAKING UNDERNEATH

PROTHONOTARY WARBLER. Only warbler with entire head and breast pure golden-yellow. Mostly yellow below, wings and closed tail uniformly blue-gray. Voice: emphatic sweet sweet sweet sweet; metallic pink. Prefers southern flooded woods. Few breed as far north as s. New Jersey, s.e. Minnesota; winters in Central and South America.

Yellowthroat

WORM-EATING WARBLER. Only warbler with four wide black stripes on olive-buff head. Bird mostly olive-brown, walks with tail well off ground. Voice: sounds like buzzy chipping sparrow. Prefers low brush on deciduous slopes. Breeds from s.w. New England, s. Iowa south to Georgia, Missouri; very few winter north to Florida.

TENNESSEE WARBLER. Male: only gray-headed warbler with conspicuous white stripe over eye. Olive-green back, white under parts. Female: head less gray, eye-stripe and under parts yellowish. Fall and immature: olive-green above, pale-yellow below, yellowish stripe over eye, faint wing-bar, white under tail. (In any plumage do not confuse with thicker-billed, stockier, slower-moving vireos.) Voice: rapid staccato *see-see see-see see-see see-see see-see-see-see-seeeeeee* (ending in trill). Prefers moist, even boggy conifer woodlands. Breeds south to n. New England, n. Minnesota; winters in Central and South America.

ORANGE-CROWNED WARBLER. Most nondescript of warblers, has **no distinctive marks.** Upper parts olive-green, under parts olive-yellow; very faint almost invisible streaks on breast; orange crown seldom noticeable. Immature and winter adults: mostly olive-green or greenish-gray above and below, faint eye-stripe, very faint breast-streaks. (Fall Tennessee lacks breast streaks, has faint wing-bar.) Voice: soft monotonous chipping sparrow-like trill. Prefers low bushy thickets. Breeds in w. Canada; migrates chiefly through central states; winters mostly in southern coastal states, vagrants occasionally as far north as Massachusetts.

NASHVILLE WARBLER. Only warbler without wing-bars having combination of **gray head, white eye-ring, yellow throat and breast.** Upper parts olive, belly whitish, rufous crown seldom visible. Female and immature: duller; eye-ring buffy. (Immature magnolia has white wing-bars and tail-band, yellow rump.) Voice: thin wiry *weesee weesee weesee chipper-chipper-chip.* Prefers moist woods or dry shrubby fields. Breeds south to n. New Jersey, Illinois; winters mostly in Central America.

KENTUCKY WARBLER. Habitually walks on ground. Mostly olive-green above, yellow underneath; **black forehead and triangular face-patches almost surround yellow spectacles.** Female and immature: paler. Voice: loud rolling *cherry-cherry-cherry-cherry-cherry.* Prefers moist deciduous woods. Breeds north to s. New York, Ohio, s. Wisconsin; winters in Mexico, Central America.

CONNECTICUT WARBLER. Male: only gray-hooded warbler with white eye-ring. Mostly olive above, yellow below.
182

(Male mourning has black breast-patch, lacks eye-ring.) Female: paler hood (white eye-ring separates it from female mourning). Immature and fall female: duskier; brown wash replaces gray hood, complete white eye-ring (immature mourning has incomplete eye-ring). Voice: loud staccato **preacher preacher preacher preacher.** Prefers moist brushy thickets (in summer conifer bogs). Breeds chiefly in Canada, some south to c. Minnesota, n. Michigan; rare in spring east of Appalachians; winters in South America.

MOURNING WARBLER. Male: only gray-hooded warbler with black patch on upper breast. Mostly olive above, yellow below (**no eye-ring** as in Connecticut). Female: paler hood without black breast-patch. Fall and immature: duskier, brown wash replaces gray hood, often incomplete eye-ring. Voice: loud musical **cherry-cherry-cherry-cherry cheer-cheer-cheer.** Prefers moist shrubby thickets. Breeds south to n. New York, c. Minnesota, in mountains to West Virginia; migrates chiefly west of Appalachians; winters in Central America.

YELLOWTHROAT (MARYLAND YELLOW-THROAT). Black mask plus bright-yellow throat of male distinctive. Mostly olive above, yellow beneath, white belly. Female: same without mask. Voice: lively **which-is-it? which-is-it? which-is-it?** or **witchity witchity witchity**; harsh scolding **chick.** Prefers dense low moist thickets. Breeds throughout; some winter, chiefly along coast south of Virginia.

YELLOW-BREASTED CHAT. Only warbler larger than song sparrow. Size, large bill and actions unwarbler-like. Throat and breast bright-yellow, upper parts uniformly olive, spectacles and belly white; long, loose tail. Voice: startling assortment of widely spaced toots, chucks, clear whistles, caws and mews. Prefers tangles of bushes and vines. Breeds north to s. New England, s. Ontario, s. Minnesota; winters in Central America.

183

HOODED WARBLER. Male: only warbler with big black hood enclosing bright-yellow cheeks and forehead. Upper parts olive-green, under parts yellow. Female: lacks hood. Both have habit of flashing white tail-spots. Voice: loud whistled **weeta weeta-you.** Prefers undergrowth in moist deciduous woods. Breeds north to Rhode Island, s. Michigan, n. Iowa; winters in Central America.

PILEOLATED WARBLER (WILSON'S). Male: only small yellow warbler with conspicuous round black cap. Olive-green above, bright-yellow beneath, black eye prominent. Female: sometimes shows suggestion of cap (immatures do not). Voice: rapid chatter **chi-chi-chi-chip-chip-chip.** Prefers swampy thickets. Breeds south to Maine, Minnesota; winters in Mexico, Central America.

CONSPICUOUS PATCHES OR BARS ON WINGS
DISTINCT STREAKING UNDERNEATH

BLACK-AND-WHITE WARBLER. Only zebra-striped warbler, even crown striped black and white; only one creeping expertly up perpendicular trunks and branches (male blackpolled has solid crown). Female and immature: paler; mostly white beneath. Voice: thin wiry **squeaky squeaky squeaky squeaky squeaky** or **we-see we-see we-see we-see we-see.** Prefers deciduous woodlands. Breeds south to n. Louisiana, Alabama; few winter north to Florida.

MAGNOLIA WARBLER. Only warbler with broad white band across black tail. Mostly gray and black above with yellow rump, conspicuous white shoulder-patches, black mask; under parts bright-yellow heavily streaked with black. Immature and fall: browner above, few streaks on yellow underparts, gray head, conspicuous eye-ring. (Tail-band, wing-bars, yellow rump distinguish it from Nashville warbler.) Voice: lively **weeta weeta weeteo;** lisping **sea-sick.** Prefers small conifers in woodlands. Breeds south to Massachusetts, Minnesota, in mountains to Virginia; winters in Central America.

CAPE MAY WARBLER. Male: only warbler with chestnut cheeks. Sides of neck, rump, under parts bright-yel-

Black-and-white Warbler

low, latter striped with black; wing-patch white; wings, back and crown dusky. Female: duller, no chestnut on cheeks. Immature and fall adults: plain olive-brown above, whitish or yellowish and heavily streaked beneath (best told by light eyestripe, yellow rump, light patch behind ear). Voice: high thin deliberate *seat seat seat seat seat.* Prefers conifers. Breeds south to Maine, New Hampshire, s. Manitoba; winters in West Indies.

MYRTLE WARBLER. Only dark looking warbler with both white throat and yellow rump. Mostly blue-gray above; white beneath with many black marks across breast; white wing-bars; yellow patch on crown, each side of breast and rump. Immature: browner, more heavily streaked, little yellow on sides. Dusky color plus yellow rump conclusive. Voice: junco-like but more warbled, rising or falling at end; harsh tchep. Prefers conifers. Breeds south to Massachusetts, Minnesota; winters chiefly in southern states, some in bayberry thickets north to Massachusetts, Ohio.

BLACK-THROATED GREEN WARBLER. Male: only black-throated warbler with olive-green crown plus bright-yellow face. Upper parts mostly olive-green, white wing-bars; under parts whitish, sides streaked with black. Female: paler; less black on throat and sides. Immature and fall adult: mostly olive-green above, white beneath, few streaks on sides, no black on throat, yellow face outlined with dusky. Voice: slow buzzy trees trees murmuring trees or see see su-zee. Prefers conifers. Breeds south to New Jersey, Ohio, in mountains to Georgia (race in cypress from Virginia to South Carolina); winters in Mexico, Central America.

CERULEAN WARBLER. Very small, some only 4¼ inches long. **Male: only warbler light-blue above, white below;** only white-breasted warbler with narrow black stripe across breast. Dark streaks on sides, white wing-bars. Female: mostly blue-gray, whitish below, two white wing-bars, pale eye-brow stripe, faint streaks on sides. Voice: rapid insect-like buzz frre frre frre freeee. Prefers deciduous woodlands. Breeds chiefly west of Appalachians from s. Ontario, s.e. Minnesota south to n. Alabama, n.e. Texas, few east to New York, Delaware; rare even on migrations east of Appalachians; winters in South America.

BLACKBURNIAN WARBLER. Male: only warbler with flaming-orange around head and throat. Mostly black and white above; conspicuous white wing-patches; black stripes across cheeks and crown; pale-yellow under parts streaked with black. Female: paler. Immature: yellow throat and breast (no orange), dark cheek-patch. Voice: thin sliding zilip zilip zilip tssssss and tzip tzip tzip tzip tssss. Prefers conifers or mixed woodlands. Breeds south to Connecticut, e. Minnesota, in mountains to Georgia; winters in South America.

YELLOW-THROATED WARBLER. Mostly gray back plus yellow throat distinctive. Under parts whitish, sides striped with black; white wing-bars and eye-stripe. Habitually creeps around branches. (Subspecies of Mississippi Valley, sycamore warbler, has yellow instead of white between eye and bill.) Voice: starts with liquid notes like waterthrush's, ends with jumpy notes like white-eyed vireo's tweet tweet tweet chick-per-wee. Prefers trees along river banks. Breeds north to Maryland, s. Wisconsin; winters north to South Carolina.

BLACKPOLLED WARBLER. Male: only warbler with solid black cap above white cheeks. Otherwise mostly gray above, white beneath; black streaks on back and sides; white wing-bars. (Black-and-white warbler has striped crown.) Female: no black cap, mostly olive-gray above, buffy-white under parts streaked with black. Fall and immature: like female but washed with yellow (resembles fall bay-breast but pale legs, white under tail). Voice: thin, wiry, staccato tsit tsit tsit tsit tsit increasing in volume in middle. Prefers conifers. Breeds south to Maine, n. New York; migrates chiefly east of Appalachians; winters in South America.

PRAIRIE WARBLER. Habitually wags tail up and down. Mostly yellow-olive above, yellow below; black streaks on sides just below wings; black stripe through eye and another across lower cheek; yellowish wing-bars. Immature: no wing-bars, faint side streaking. Voice: evenly spaced, ascending, buzzy zee zee zee zee zee. Prefers pine and scrub oak barrens. Breeds north to Massachusetts, Ohio, locally farther; winters in West Indies, few north to Florida.

187

GOLDEN-WINGED WARBLER. Only warbler having both black throat and golden wing-patch. Mostly gray above, white below, yellow forehead, black eye-patch. Female: black replaced by gray. Voice: buzzy zee bzz bzz bzz. Prefers brushy clearings near woods. Breeds from c. New England, c. Minnesota, south to New Jersey, Iowa, in mountains to Georgia; migrates through gulf states to tropics.

BLUE-WINGED WARBLER. Only warbler with bright-yellow under parts and head plus narrow black stripe through eye. Back olive-yellow, wings blue-gray barred with white. Female and immature: duller. Voice: buzzy oh-geee or zee zoo. Prefers brushy fields. Breeds from s. New England, s. Minnesota south to Delaware, Kansas, in mountains to Georgia; migrates through gulf states to tropics.

PARULA WARBLER. Only bluish warbler with yellow throat and breast. Very small (4¼ inches long); broad white wing-bars, yellowish patch on back. Male: red wash across yellow breast. Voice: sizzling insect-like trill running up scale tumbling at end ffrrrrrup! orfr fr fr frrrrrup! Breeds chiefly in usnea lichen and Spanish moss (locally elsewhere) north to Gulf of St. Lawrence, Minnesota; some winter in Florida.

BLACK-THROATED BLUE WARBLER. Male: only warbler with dark gray-blue back plus black throat and sides. Under parts white, small white square in wing. Female: mostly olive-brown with white eye-stripe, white square in wing. Voice: slow hummed buzz increasing in volume zoo zoo zoo zee. Prefers rich undergrowth in woodlands. Breeds from s. Quebec, n. Minnesota south to n. Connecticut, c. Minnesota, in mountains to Georgia; winters chiefly in West Indies.

CHESTNUT-SIDED WARBLER. Only warbler with yellow cap plus chestnut sides. Back mostly bright olive-green, under parts white; wing-bars yellow; two black stripes across face joining at bill. Fall and immature: mostly yellow-green

Blue-winged Warbler

above, white below, white eye-ring. Voice: cheerful *I'm very pleased to meetcha;* a longer complicated warble. Prefers shrubby fields. Breeds south to New Jersey, Ohio, Nebraska, in mountains to South Carolina; winters in Central America.

BAY-BREASTED WARBLER. Male: only dark looking warbler with chestnut on sides, breast, throat, head. Back mostly dark-gray, under parts whitish; buffy patch on side of neck; white wing-bars. Female: chestnut mostly replaced by gray. Fall and immature: mostly olive above, buffy below (even under tail), black legs (blackpolled has pale legs, white under tail). Voice: high thin *teasy teasy teasy teasy*. Prefers conifers. Breeds south to n. New York, n. Minnesota; winters in Central and South America.

PINE WARBLER. Clings and creeps on trunks and branches more than any other yellowish warbler. Mostly dusky-yellow above, bright-yellow throat and breast, the latter faintly streaked; conspicuous white wing-bars, yellow eye-strip. Voice: trill slower and more musical than chipping sparrow's. Prefers pine woods. Breeds locally almost throughout; winters chiefly in southern states.

AMERICAN REDSTART. Male: our only warbler that looks all coal-black and bright orange-red. Mostly black; belly white; orange-red on wing-stripes, sides of breast, sides of tail. Very animated, flycatches, constantly fans tail and wings. Female: mostly gray above, white below, orange-red replaced by yellow. Voice: weak sibilant see-see-see see sée; also chewee chewee chewee. Prefers second growth deciduous woods. Breeds south to n. Georgia, Louisiana; winters in tropics.

HOUSE SPARROW
Passerinæ

House Sparrow

THE WELL-KNOWN house sparrow or English sparrow is not a sparrow at all but belongs to an Old World Family called weaver finches. This foreign family is so large, diversified and complicated that it would serve little purpose to analyze it here. Since their introduction into New York City in 1850 house sparrows have increased tremendously and spread over most of the United States and southern Canada. Everyone knows these bustling, perky, high-strung, aggressive residents of city streets and farmyards. They are the size of song sparrows, have short thick bills, habitually flick their tails and produce a repetitious throaty **chee-ip**. Although they spend a great deal of time feeding on the ground they hop, never walk. The male is brown above, gray-white below and has a black throat, gray crown, white cheeks and chestnut nape. The female is dull-brown above, gray-white below, and has a pale stripe over each eye. In most areas these birds nest in bird houses, sheds or crevices in buildings, but in some sections they build large round grassy nests with small entrances at the side. In some regions they gather in great nocturnal roosts, one such roost I have studied in El Paso, Texas, consisting of thousands of birds.

BLACKBIRDS
Icteridæ (in part)

Redwing

THE MEMBERS of this large diversified family are so varied that it is difficult to give any field characteristics that will cover all. They range in length from the six inch orchard oriole to the seventeen inch male boat-tailed grackle. They all have flat foreheads, strong sharply pointed bills and produce harsh chattering scolds. Although they spend a great deal of time in trees and bushes, most of them are primarily terrestrial, walking about gracefully in search of food. Field students often find it convenient to separate them into three distinct groups: the orioles which are brightly colored arboreal blackbirds are treated separately. The meadowlarks are short-tailed, plump, almost round, and in flight resemble large-breasted starlings with a characteristic hesitant flight produced by a few rapid wing-beats and a sail. The rest which most people visualize when one says 'blackbirds' are mostly black, well proportioned and have ample to long tails. Outside the breeding season they are decidedly gregarious, some winter roosts often numbering one hundred thousand or more. Some are gregarious throughout the year, often nesting in sizable colonies. The flight of the large grackles is usually steady and direct, that of the smaller species distinctly undulating.

Many people erroneously assume that the black crows and starlings belong to the blackbird family, but each of these birds is in a distinct family of its own. Crows are much larger, stockier and heavier-billed. Starlings are shorter-tailed than any dark blackbird and have a distinctive bustling gait.

BOBOLINK. Male: our only song bird, black below, largely white above. Smaller than robin. Dark wings and upper back, black face, yellowish-buff nape. Female, immature and fall male: mostly brownish-yellow; dark stripes on head, back and sides. Voice: startling, bubbling, tinkling **rob-rob Lincoln-Lincoln bobolink bobolink bobolink spink-spank-spink** often delivered in flight as bird quivers on vibrant downward pointed wings; metallic **peenk.** Prefers meadows. Breeds south to New Jersey, Illinois, Missouri (accidental on migrations in southwest); winters in South America.

COMMON MEADOWLARK. Robin size, chunky, short-tailed; brown above, yellow below, black V on breast, white outer tail feathers, black stripes on head. Nervously flicks tail as it walks. Its flight, several short rapid wing-beats followed by a sail is unmistakable. Voice: loud, clear, whistled spring-o-the-year; abrupt z-d-t. Prefers grassy fields and meadows. Breeds locally almost throughout; winters chiefly in southern states (replaced westward on plains by similar looking western meadowlark having richer bubbling song).

YELLOW-HEADED BLACKBIRD. Male: only black bird with bright-yellow head. Robin size, white patches on wings. Female: smaller, browner, paler-yellow confined to face, throat, chest. Voice: startling wonk wonk wonk followed by squeaky crackling noises; harsh chuck. Prefers fresh water marshes. Breeds very locally east to Wisconsin, Iowa, Indiana; some winter in southernmost states west of the Mississippi.

REDWING (RED-WINGED BLACKBIRD). Male: only black bird in East with bright-red shoulder-patches. Slightly smaller than robin, flirts tail when excited. Red patches often concealed, only yellow border showing. Immature male: dark-brown, heavily streaked, dull-red shoulder-patches. Female and young: gray-brown, heavily streaked. Voice: liquid, gurgling qonk-la-ree; harsh check. Prefers marshes, moist meadows. Breeds throughout; winters mostly south of New York and Ohio.

RUSTY BLACKBIRD. Robin-sized black bird with yellow-white eyes. Male: black, green gloss about head. Female: dark-brown and gray. Immature and fall adults: brown with rusty barring. Voice: squeaks like rusty hinge do-oil-me; harsh check. Prefers flooded woodlands. Breeds south to n. New York; winters chiefly in southern states.

BOAT-TAILED GRACKLE. Largest of blackbirds. Male: often 17 inches long; glossy-black, long tail creased down center. Female: only 13 inches long; chiefly brown.

Voice: amazing variety of whistles, squeaks, metallic crackles. Prefers marshes (outside Florida mostly salt marshes). Resident along coast from Delaware to Texas.

PURPLE GRACKLE (Crow-Blackbird). Foot long iridescent black bird with long tail, graceful stride, pale-yellow eye. In sunlight often quite purple, blue or bronze. Tail of spring male shows V-shaped crease. Voice: harsh squeaks like rusty hinge (produced with much effort); harsh chuck. Prefers extensive lawns in parks, cemeteries, gardens. Breeds locally throughout; winters chiefly in southern states.

BROWN-HEADED COWBIRD. Male: only black bird with brown head. Black plumage glossed with blue or green. Smaller than robin, bill short for a blackbird, walks with tail well off ground. **Female:** mostly gray. Voice: bubbling, liquid blub-blub-blee given with spread of wings; harsh check; high whistled zeee ti-ti. Breeds south to Virginia, Tennessee, Mexico; winters chiefly in southern states.

ORIOLES
Icteridæ (in part)

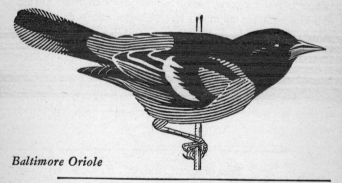

Baltimore Oriole

NEW WORLD orioles are brightly colored arboreal blackbirds. Like all members of their family they have flat foreheads and strong sharply pointed bills. Unlike other blackbirds they seldom come to the ground and most species show little or no gregarious tendencies. Their long neatly woven nests usually are suspended from the tip of a branch. Although their harsh chattering scolds are quite similar to those of other blackbirds they are good singers, producing a variety of clear whistles and sweet rich warbles.

BALTIMORE ORIOLE. Male: only almost robin-sized orange and black bird over most of East. Under parts, rump, shoulders and sides of tail brilliant-orange; head, upper back, most of wings and tail black; wing-bar and wing-edgings white. Female: dull-yellow above, orange-yellow below, two white wing-bars. Voice: loud clear whistled surely; song: sure-ly sure-ly sure-ly sure-ly-the-world-is-bright-and-gay. Prefers tall trees in towns and open country. Breeds south to inland Georgia and Texas (accidental along s.e. coast); winters in Central America.

ORCHARD ORIOLE. Distinctly smaller than robin. Male: our only dark-looking oriole. Similar pattern to preceding but under parts, rump and shoulders chestnut instead of brilliant-orange; tail mostly black. Female: chiefly dull-yellow; gray wings and back, two white wing-bars. Young male: similar to female but throat black. Voice: loud rapid warble. Prefers gardens and orchards. Breeds north to s. New England, Michigan, Minnesota; winters in Central America.

TANAGERS
Thraupidæ

THIS distinctly American family is very closely allied to the finches. Its members are strictly arboreal and usually are found in woodlands. Our species are larger than a song sparrow and much heavier. They are stocky but well proportioned and possess a slightly forked tail of medium length, and a rather thick medium-length bill with the upper mandible slightly notched. There are marked external sexual differences, the males being strikingly brilliant, the females much more

Scarlet Tanager

modestly colored. Tanagers are deliberate, almost vireo-like in actions, slowly weaving their heads from side to side as they methodically search twigs and leaves for insects.

The only resemblance our male tanagers have to a cardinal is in color. The large conical bill and crested head of the cardinal are usually so obvious that there is no reason for confusion. Yellow female tanagers superficially resemble female orioles but orioles are much slimmer, longer-tailed and have very sharply pointed untanager-like bills.

SCARLET TANAGER. Male: our only scarlet bird with black wings and tail. Female: dull greenish-yellow above, yellow below, dark-gray wings. Fall males: scarlet gradually replaced by patches of yellow-green. Voice: short, slow, high-pitched, robin-like **cheer-up cheerily cheer-up cheer-up** (sounds as though bird were whistling and humming at the same time—robin with a sore throat); low **chip-churr.** Prefers deciduous woods. Breeds south to n. Georgia and Kansas; winters in South America.

SUMMER TANAGER. Male: our only pure red bird without a crest. Female: olive-yellow above, orange-yellow below. Changing males: patched red and greenish-yellow. Voice: song not as clear and lively as robin's, not as short and hoarse as scarlet tanager's; snappy **pick-up**; chattery **chicky-tucky-tuck.** Prefers open dry woods. Breeds north to Delaware, Ohio, s.e. Wisconsin; winters in Central and South America.

SPARROW FAMILY (GROSBEAKS, FINCHES,
Fringillidæ SPARROWS, BUNTINGS)

Vesper Sparrow

THIS largest family of birds in the world is considered by many scientists to consist of the most highly developed of all birds. They are widely diversified in form, actions and habitat preference, but they all have stout, conical bills adapted for cracking seeds. There is an amazing variety of bills; small, stout and triangular in the finches, buntings and sparrows; large, thick and rounded in the cardinals and grosbeaks; crossed at the tips in the crossbills. The majority of the brightly colored finches, buntings and grosbeaks are chiefly arboreal; most of the brown sparrows essentially terrestrial. Some of our finest singers are included in this family. Many of the sparrows are so shy, retiring and difficult to study and so closely resemble other related species that they are often extremely difficult to identify.

CARDINAL. Male: our only red bird with crest. Size of small robin. Face black around base of large conical red bill. Female: crested; yellow-brown with red wash; red bill. Voice: clear whistled **birdy birdy birdy** and **sweet sweet sweet whatcheer what-cheer what-cheer sweet sweet sweet;** dry tip. Prefers bushy thickets in towns or open country. Resident east of plains, north to southern parts of New York, Ontario, Minnesota.

ROSE-BREASTED GROSBEAK. Male: only bird with bright-red triangular patch on white breast. Smaller than robin, very large conical whitish bill. Head, back, wings and tail mostly black, under parts and rump mostly white; wing-bars and wing-patch white. Female: chiefly brown heavily streaked; broad whitish stripe over eye, white wing-bars, orange under wings. Fall males: brownish on upper parts and breast, red wash on breast and under wings. Voice: sweet, short, bubbling, robin-like song with much swing, practically no pauses: **Oh what joy. I'm bubbling o'er with bubbling joy;** metallic chink. Prefers open thickets near low moist woodlands. Breeds from s. Quebec and c. Manitoba south to New Jersey, Kansas, in mountains to Georgia; winters in Central and South America.

BLUE GROSBEAK. Male: our only thick-billed, mostly dark-blue bird (often appears black). Larger, chunkier, shorter-tailed than song sparrow. Brown wing-bars. (Indigo bunting much smaller, tiny-billed; brown on wings of young males not so sharply defined.) Female: mostly gray-brown above, smooth pale-brown below, **two brown wing-bars.** (Large size, chunky shape, big bill and conspicuous wing-bars separate it from female indigo bunting.) Immature male: like female but washed with blue. Voice: quick throaty rising and falling two-note warbles; snappy chink. Prefers brushy thickets. Breeds very locally north to Maryland, Illinois; winters in Central America (accidental in northeast, most reports referable to young male indigo buntings).

INDIGO BUNTING. Male: our only small, tiny-billed, mostly deep-blue bird (looks black at a distance). Size of small song sparrow with short tail, tiny triangular bill. Female: uniform brown (size, shape, tiny bill, lack of any obvious marks or patches identifies it). Fall and immature males: varying amounts of blue and brown (see blue grosbeak). Voice: high varied notes usually in twos: **sweet-sweet chip-chip chee-chee sweet-sweet eat-eat, or fire-fire where-where here-here let's-put-it-out!** Prefers brushy thickets near deciduous woods. Breeds from s. New Brunswick and North Dakota south to c. Georgia, Louisiana, Texas; winters mostly in tropics.

PAINTED BUNTING. Male: our most colorful bird. Under parts and rump bright-red, head blue, back green. Size of small song sparrow, tiny triangular bill. Female: green above, yellow-green below. Voice: sweet lively warbles; sharp chip. Prefers brushy thickets. Breeds north to s.e. North Carolina, Kansas; some winter as far north as southern half of Florida.

DICKCISSEL. Male: suggests house sparrow with meadowlark's breast. Mostly gray-brown above, chestnut patch on shoulder, yellow breast, black patch on chest, yellowish stripe over eye. Female: like female house sparrow but yellow wash on breast and eye-stripe. Voice: emphatic, sharp **dick dick ciss-ciss-cissel.** Prefers extensive prairies or cultivated fields. Breeds chiefly on prairies, some east to s. Michigan, south to Alabama, Texas; winters in South America.

EVENING GROSBEAK. Male: only yellow song bird with very large thick-based whitish bill. Shorter than robin and chubbier with short notched tail. Mostly yellow; black wings, tail, and crown; large white wing-patch. Female; similar shape and pattern but paler, yellow mostly replaced by gray. Voice: shrill **chee-ip**; sweet wandering warble. Breeds south east to n. Michigan (few to n. New York, n. Maine); winters south irregularly to New Jersey, Kentucky, Missouri, occasionally farther.

PURPLE FINCH. Song sparrow size; conical bill, short notched tail. **Male: color of raspberry stain, brightest on head and rump.** Female: mostly brown, heavily streaked; light stripe over eye, brown patches on cheek and side of throat. Voice: loud bubbling warble; soft **tick tick.** Prefers evergreens. Breeds south to n. New Jersey, n. Illinois, in mountains to Maryland; winters almost throughout, mostly in southern states.

PINE GROSBEAK. Robin-sized finch with short, thick, rounded bill, medium-lengthed notched tail, conspicuous white wing-bars. Male: dark rose-red; black wings and tail, two white or pale-rose wing-bars. (Purple finch: sparrow-sized, small bill, dull wing-bars. White-winged crossbill much smaller, crossed bill.) Female: mostly buffy-gray; greenish-yellow wash on head and rump, black wings and tail, white wing-bars. (Evening grosbeak: stockier, shorter-tailed, larger-billed, large white wing-patches.) Immature male: like female but red wash on head and rump. Voice: clear whistled **you-you-you;** loud musical whistles and warbles suggesting cross between robin and purple finch songs. Prefers edges of conifer woodlands, in winter frequently feeds on sumach and mountain ash. Resident in Canada, few south to highlands of Maine and New Hampshire; irregular winter flights to New Jersey, Ohio, rarely farther.

COMMON REDPOLL. Only small finch with red forehead and black chin. Smaller than song sparrow; size, shape and actions very similar to goldfinch's. Mostly gray-brown and heavily streaked above; paler under parts, streaked sides. Male: rosy wash to breast. Immature: grayer; more heavily streaked above and below. Voice: rattling **chif-chif** drier more rolling than call of white-winged crossbill; goldfinch-like dee-ar; sweet rippling trreerree. Prefers bush-stippled fields and swamps. Breeds chiefly in subarctic; irregular winter visitor to northern states, rarely south to North Carolina, Oklahoma.

PINE SISKIN. Smaller than song sparrow, tiny pointed bill, short notched tail. Mostly gray-brown, heavily and uniformly streaked with olive-brown, some yellow on wings and tail. Voice: husky clear-it; rising shreee. Prefers conifers. Breeds south to New England, Minnesota, in mountains to North Carolina; winters erratically and locally, usually north of Florida, c. Louisiana.

AMERICAN GOLDFINCH. Male: only small bright-yellow bird with black wings, tail and forehead. Often called wild canary. Size of small song sparrow, small triangular bill; short notched tail; distinctive up-and-down roller-coaster flight. Female and winter male: mostly dull-yellow, dark wings, white wing-bars. Voice: long sweet musical song; canary-like swee-eeee; in flight whistled per-chick-o-ree often given at each crest. Prefers shrubby fields and meadows. Breeds from s. Canada south to n. Georgia, s. Oklahoma; winters locally throughout, mostly in southern states.

RED CROSSBILL. This and following species our only birds with crossed mandibles. Usually found clinging near conifer cones, expertly extracting seeds with their unique bills. Red crossbill our only crossbill without wing-bars. Song sparrow size. Male: dark-red with dark-brown wings and tail (bird often appears black). Female: olive-buff with dusky wings, tail and back, yellowish rump. Young male: patched buff and red with dusky wings and tail. Juvenile: mostly grayish, heavily streaked; resembles large heavy-billed siskin. Voice: sharp jip-jip; rich musical trills and warbles. Prefers conifers, especially spruce. Resident chiefly in Canada, some south to evergreen woodlands of northernmost states, few occasionally breed south to North Carolina; rare erratic winter visitor south to Florida and Texas.

WHITE-WINGED CROSSBILL. Only crossbill with white wing-bars. Size of song sparrow. Male: deep rosy-pink with black wings and tail, broad white wing-bars. Female: mostly olive-buff with blackish wings, back and tail, yellowish rump, broad white wing-bars. Young male: patched buff and reddish, dark wings and tail, white wing-bars. Juvenile: mostly grayish, heavily streaked, white wing-bars. Voice: unmusical chif-chif, musical peet; loud rich canary-like trills, often delivered as bird flutters above tree tops. Prefers conifers, especially spruce (feeding on cones). Resident chiefly in Canada, some south to evergreen woodlands of northernmost states (unpredictable wanderings around breeding range); periodic light winter flights south to North Carolina and Kansas.

EASTERN TOWHEE. Slightly smaller than robin; habitually scratches among leaves. Often called ground robin despite white breast, sparrow shape and mannerisms. Male: hood and upper parts black; under parts white, sides chestnut-red, eyes red; long rounded black tail habitually fanned showing white outer-tips. Female: similar, black replaced by brown. Voice: slow sweet drink-your-teaeeee or see tow-hee ending with trill; sharp chewink. (White-eyed subspecies occurring in Florida and along coast to North Carolina often called joree because of high-pitched scolding joree; its song a less accented cheap cheap cheese.) Prefers brushy thickets, especially in open woodlands. Breeds from s. Maine, s. Ontario, s. Manitoba south to Florida; winters chiefly in southern states.

SAVANNAH SPARROW. Like song sparrow but short notched tail, yellow wash in eye-stripe; stripe through crown, breast-button small. Voice: comparable to thin-voiced high-pitched buzzy song sparrow: sip sip sip sip-tea teateeea. Prefers grassy meadows. Breeds south to New Jersey, Indiana, Missouri; winters chiefly south of breeding range.

IPSWICH SPARROW. Large pale edition of savannah sparrow (possibly only a subspecies) found on grassy coastal sand dunes. Size of large song sparrow. Breeds on Sable

202

Island, Nova Scotia; migrates along narrow coastal strip (accidental elsewhere); winters on grassy coastal sand dunes, chiefly from New Jersey to Georgia.

GRASSHOPPER SPARROW. Small short-tailed brown sparrow with large flat head, light stripe through dark crown, heavily streaked back, unstreaked buff-washed under parts. (See Henslow's sparrow.) Voice: insect-like buzz get-up geeeee. Prefers dry weedy fields and prairies. Breeds locally north to c. New England and Minnesota; winters in southern states.

HENSLOW'S SPARROW. Small short-tailed flat-headed large-billed sparrow usually found in weed-choked fields. Size and shape plus rusty wings, black-striped olive head, finely streaked breast and sides conclusive. Smaller than song sparrow, size of grasshopper sparrow. Upper parts mostly brown with black-striped back; under parts buffy-white, finely streaked on breast and sides. (Grasshopper sparrow lacks rusty wings and fine streaking on breast.) Immature: duller, few streaks on breast. (Separated from grasshopper chiefly by rusty wash on wings.) Voice: weak ridiculous sea-sick. Breeds from s. New England, s. Ontario, South Dakota south to North Carolina and Texas; winters chiefly in southeastern states.

SHARP-TAILED SPARROW. Yellow-tan wash on head surrounding dark cheek-patch identifies this salt-marsh dweller. Size of small song sparrow with short pointed tail. Mostly brown; streaked back, breast and sides. Voice: buzzy cut-up cheese. Breeds locally in tidal marshes from Gulf of St. Lawrence south to Virginia; winters in similar habitat chiefly south of Connecticut. It is far too risky for most field students to separate the five geographical races, although one breeding locally in fresh water marshes from Minnesota to Great Slave Lake is usually buffier with few breast-streaks.

SEASIDE SPARROW. Dingy colorless salt marsh sparrow with noticeably large bill, yellow streak before eye.

Song sparrow size. Mostly drab olive-gray, indistinctly streaked. Voice: buzzy cut-up-the-cheese; harsh check. Breeds locally in coastal salt marshes from Massachusetts to Texas; few winter north of Delaware.

VESPER SPARROW. Quite similar to song sparrow but grayer, conspicuous white outer tail feathers, chestnut shoulder-patch, pale eye-ring, no breast-spot. Voice: richer, more mellow than song sparrow's, starting with two low sweet whistles. Prefers dry grassy fields and prairies. Breeds from s. Canada south to North Carolina, Missouri, Texas; winters chiefly in southern states.

LARK SPARROW. Only sparrow with bold chestnut cheek-patches and head-stripes. Song sparrow size. Mostly brown above, pale-gray beneath; dark spot in center of unstreaked breast, dark fan-shaped tail with much white on outer tips. Immature: duller; no breast-spot, delicate streaks instead. Voice: series of sweet rich warbles and trills. Prefers pastures and sparsely coated fields. Breeds from s. Ontario, Minnesota, south to Louisiana, Texas; winters in Gulf States; very rare visitor east of Appalachians.

BACHMAN'S SPARROW (PINEWOODS). Might be described as drab-colored field sparrow without wing-bars, without warm browns, with rounded rather than notched tail, dark instead of pink bill. Size of song sparrow. Mostly drab-brown above, dark stripes on back, dull buffy cast to unstreaked breast, pale stripe over eye, light throat. Secretive, difficult to study. Voice: sweet refrain of whistles and trills. Prefers undergrowth in open pine or oak woods. Breeds north to Maryland, Illinois, s.e. Iowa; winters chiefly in southernmost states.

SLATE-COLORED JUNCO. Our only dark smooth slate-gray sparrow with contrasting white lower breast and belly. Size of song sparrow. White outer tail feathers, pink bill. Immature: browner. Juvenile: brownish-gray; streaked.

(Vesper sparrow richer brown, avoids woodlands.) Voice: slow, tinkling chipping sparrow-like trill; sweet twitters; soft musical smack. Prefers conifer woodlands. Breeds south to Maine, Michigan and Minnesota, in mountains to Georgia; common winter resident almost throughout.

TREE SPARROW. Resembles large brown chipping sparrow but has **dark central breast-spot,** yellow lower mandible, no distinct white stripe over eye. (**Chestnut cap, dark breast-spot, white wing-bars conclusive.**) Voice: thin tseet; sweet tinkling teelweet. Prefers weedy open country. Breeds mostly in Arctic; winter visitor (chiefly from late October to late March) south to South Carolina, Arkansas.

CHIPPING SPARROW. Only small chestnut-capped sparrow with conspicuous black line through and white stripe above eye. Smaller than song sparrow. Back brownish, under parts plain pale-gray, bill dark. Immature: buffier; streaked dull-brown crown; brown cheek-patch, gray rump. Juvenile: finely streaked below. Voice: sharp chip; simple trill on one pitch, resembling sound from small toy sewing machine. Prefers gardens, farmlands, country roadsides. Breeds from s. Canada south to South Carolina, Alabama, c. Texas; winters chiefly in southern states. (Most winter reports from northern states undoubtedly referable to tree sparrow.)

CLAY-COLORED SPARROW. Very similar to immature chipping sparrow but more sharply defined gray-brown cheek-patch, whiter eye-stripe, paler bill, obvious light stripe through crown. Immature: browner (safely separated from immature chippy only by buff instead of gray rump). Voice: soft chip; slow unmusical buzzing **bzz-zz-zz-zz-zz.** Prefers brushy thickets. Breeds in interior south to northern parts of Nebraska, Iowa, and Illinois, some east to c. Michigan (migrants accidental east of Appalachians); winters chiefly in Mexico.

FIELD SPARROW. Resembles very brown-backed chipping sparrow but has all **pink bill, brown wash on breast,**

sides and cheeks; no conspicuous black or white stripe over eye. Narrow eye-ring usually obvious. (Tree sparrow has breast-spot, dark upper mandible, grayer cheeks and nape.) Juvenile: finely streaked below. Voice: sweet, clear, piping ter-wee ter-wee ter-wee te de-de-de-de-de; soft tsip. Prefers brushy fields and pastures. Breeds from s. Quebec, s. Minnesota south to n. Florida, n.e. Mexico; winters chiefly in southern half of U.S.

HARRIS' SPARROW. Our only large sparrow with black crown, face, throat and upper breast. Much larger and heavier than song sparrow; fox sparrow size. Mostly brown above, pale-gray below, gray sides to head, reddish bill. (Breeding-plumaged Lapland longspur has black crown, face and throat but is much smaller with rusty nape, black stripe down side.) Winter adults: crown and chest grayer. Immature: buffier, especially on face; crown gray-brown, no black around bill and throat, black streaks across chest, pink bill (second year birds some black on throat and crown). Voice: loud scolding wink; clear plaintive whistles. Prefers low brushy thickets with scattering of trees. Breeds mostly between Hudson Bay and Great Slave Lake; migrates chiefly through prairie states, few east to Ohio (accidentally east of Appalachians); winters from s. Nebraska to Texas.

WHITE-CROWNED SPARROW. Raised crown broadly striped with black and white plus reddish bill conclusive. Larger than song sparrow. Brown back, clear pale-gray breast. (See white-throated sparrow.) Immature: washed with brown; bill pink, head stripes brown and light buff. Voice: sharp chip; soft plaintive pee bee bee bee chee zee-zee. Prefers brushy thickets. Breeds in Canada; transient in northern states; winters chiefly in southern states (uncommon east of Appalachians).

WHITE-THROATED SPARROW. Similar to preceding but grayer-breasted, conspicuous sharply defined white throat, flatter head, yellow between eye and dark bill. The head
206

is just as boldly striped black and white as in the white-crowned. Immature: duskier; streaked breast; head-stripes dark-brown and buff; smaller duller throat-patch, dark bill. Voice: clear, slow, high-pitched whistled I sing plaintively plaintively plaintively; lisping tsit. Prefers brushy thickets in or around open woodlands. Breeds south to n. New England, c. Minnesota, in mountains to Pennsylvania; winters chiefly in southern states, few north to Massachusetts, Ohio.

FOX SPARROW. Our only large, chubby, reddish-brown sparrow; larger, stockier than song sparrow. Mostly brown; reddish-brown on tail, wings and the numerous breast-stripes. Habitually scratches in leaves. (Hermit thrush has rusty tail, but is duller brown, spotted instead of streaked beneath, and has more upright military thrush posture and actions.) Voice: long tssip; loud smack; loud beautiful whistled melody hear hear I-sing-sweet sweeter most-sweetly. Prefers brushy woodland thickets. Breeds in Canada; migrates across northern states, most wintering south of Connecticut, Ohio, Iowa.

LINCOLN'S SPARROW. Resembles small, trim, gray-brown song sparrow with very fine black streaking underneath, light buffy wash across breast; some with central breast-spot. (Immature song and swamp sparrows quite similar but Lincoln's is always grayer-backed with finer streaking below, more strongly striped crown.) Shy and difficult to study. Voice: sharp chup; soft sweet bubbling warble. Prefers moist thickets, especially bordering swampy woodlands. Breeds mostly in Canada, some south to northernmost U.S.; winters from Mississippi and Oklahoma south to Guatemala.

SWAMP SPARROW. Dark-brown marsh dweller with chestnut cap, whitish throat, gray breast and cheeks, faintly streaked sides. Slightly smaller than song sparrow. Immature: duskier; head brownish, dull blurred streaks on buffy breast. Voice: tweet-tweet-tweet-tweet, etc; slower, louder, more metallic trill than chipping sparrow's; metallic chip. Prefers fresh water marshes, swamps. Breeds locally south to New Jersey, West Virginia, Missouri; winters chiefly south of breeding range to Gulf of Mexico.

SONG SPARROW. Our most common and widely distributed sparrow. Length 5–6¾ inches. Mostly brown above, buffy-white below; heavily streaked with dark-brown above and below; long rounded tail, conspicuous spot or "Audubon Club button" in center of breast. Young: finely streaked below, breast-spot often lacking. Voice: loud tchunk; lively sweet Madge Madge Madge put-on-your-tea-kettle. Prefers brushy thickets, shrubbery in gardens. Breeds south to North Carolina, n. Georgia, Missouri; winters almost throughout, most south of Massachusetts, Michigan, Iowa.

LAPLAND LONGSPUR. Longspurs are sparrowlike birds with long hind toes, inhabiting plains and barren fields. Unlike sparrows they walk and run more frequently than hop. Lapland is only longspur occuring regularly east of the Mississippi. Size of large song sparrow. Summer male: only longspur with mostly black face and throat. Chiefly brownish above, whitish below, chestnut nape, white wing-bars; black on crown, face, throat and stripe down side. Winter birds (plumage usually seen in our region): mostly streaked gray-brown above, buffy-white below; white wing-bars, dark streaks on sides, rusty wash to nape and wings, dusky cheek-patch; usually dark smudge on chest; white on outer tail feathers. Voice: harsh rattling chirr; musical dicky-dick chew chew. Breeds in Arctic; winters mostly on plains south to Texas; rare east of Illinois. (Eastern stragglers usually found in flocks of snow buntings and horned larks.)

SNOW BUNTING. Name describes bird: in flight looks mostly white; on ground, brown and white with large white wing-patches. Slightly larger and much stouter than song sparrow. Walks and runs, seldom hops. Gregarious; often in flocks of several hundred. Voice: clear whistled here; cheerful chirrirrip. Prefers wide open rather barren treeless country. Breeds in Arctic; winter visitor to northern states, occasionally south to North Carolina, Kansas.

INDEX